Clapham 2004

Emma,
 Hope this book is useful as you go
off to Uni. It's been great having
you in the tent ... well done camper-
of-the-year !
     love from
         Jo.

Has science got rid of God?

Emma, ☺
   Thank-you for being a "bubbly"
tent member - you've been
great!
   Hope this book may provide
you with some useful discussion
points.
        God Bless,
          Love Chaa
               x x
             x x

£1.50

Has science got rid of God?

John Blanchard

EVANGELICAL PRESS

EVANGELICAL PRESS
Faverdale North Industrial Estate, Darlington, DL3 0PH, England

Evangelical Press USA
P. O. Box 825, Webster, New York 14580, USA

e-mail: sales@evangelicalpress.org
web: http://www.evangelicalpress.org

First published 2004

British Library Cataloguing in Publication Data available

ISBN 0 85234 568 2

Other books by John Blanchard

Does God Believe in Atheists?	*Truth for Life*
Evolution — True or False?	*Ultimate Questions*
How to Enjoy your Bible	*What in the World is a Christian?*
Is God Past his Sell-by Date?	*Whatever Happened to Hell?*
Meet the Real Jesus	*Where was God on September 11?*
Read Mark Learn	*Why Believe the Bible?*
Right with God	

Printed and bound in Great Britain by Creative Print & Design Wales, Ebbw Vale

Contents

Preface

Science and religion are two of the most pervasive influences the world has ever known and they affect virtually every person now living on our planet. If I key the word 'Science' into my favourite internet search engine it offers me 62,300,000 pages to browse; when I try 'Religion' another 18,500,000 pages are available. If my search combines the two words I am still faced with 3,270,000 sites crammed with facts and figures, claims and counter-claims, ideas and opinions.

For many people, combining the two is precisely the problem, as they are often held to be diametrically opposed to each other. Writing in 1980, the British scientist Edgar Andrews, Emeritus Professor of Materials in the University of London, began an excellent book on the subject with the words: 'The divorce between science and religion is one of the most significant aspects of our modern philosophical scene.'[1] There are times when this 'divorce' expresses itself in a kind of 'cold war', with both sides ignoring each other. At other times the 'hot war' spills across the media, sometimes sparked by such things as a new scientific discovery, an exciting archaeological 'find', a medical breakthrough that raises moral or ethical issues, or the educational establishment's way of teaching about the origins of the world or of the human race.

The idea that science and religion are in conflict has had a long shelf life, dating at least from the last third of the nineteenth century, but does it have any solid basis? Are we forced to take one side or the other? Must we accept that they will always be at loggerheads? Is there no case for saying that each has a valid part to play in our understanding of reality and in our daily experience?

I am grateful to Professor Edgar Andrews, Dr Andrew Blanchard, Dr Andy Christofides, Steve Layfield, the Rev. Philip Miller and Professor Colin Runciman for their kind help in reviewing the manuscript and making suggestions for its correction and improvement; they are in no way responsible for any weaknesses that remain. My long-time secretary, Joy Harling, did her usual excellent work in preparing the material for the publisher.

If you are looking for a comprehensive examination of these questions that delves into every nook and cranny of scientific discovery and expounds the depths of religious thought over the centuries you will obviously need to look elsewhere — including those millions of internet pages! The book you are holding is nothing more than a basic outline of the fundamental issues involved, yet I believe it points to there being a clear and convincing answer to the question posed in the title.

John Blanchard
Banstead
Surrey
April 2004

1.
Fine-tuning the question

Let me come clean. I am neither a scientist nor the son of a scientist. I do have a son with two earned scientific degrees, a B.Sc. in genetics and a Ph.D. in molecular biology, but other than making my normal genetic contribution to his make-up some twenty years before he achieved the first of these distinctions, I can claim no credit for either of them. After I had spoken at Cambridge University recently an undergraduate asked me, 'What is your background in science?' In reply, I told him that in formal terms I had none and that I could almost relate to Archbishop William Temple's confession: 'My ignorance of science is so profound as to be distinguished!'[1] This may seem an unpromising start, but half a century of fascination with the subject, fuelled by countless hours of reading, discussion and note-taking, to say nothing of access to a cascade of information on the internet, provides more than enough expert information and analysis to offer a straightforward answer to the question posed in the book's title. I will also lean gently on the ancient claim that theology is 'the Queen of the sciences'!

First things first: what does 'science' mean? The word has roots in Middle English, Old French and Latin, in which *scientia* is based on a verb meaning 'to know'. So far so good, but as the American scholar J. P. Moreland points out, 'No generally accepted definition of what science is is agreed on by a majority of philosophers of science... There are some cases of what most people would consider to be science, but there does not seem to be an adequate definition of science which covers all the cases.'[2] 'Science' used to mean nothing more than 'knowledge', but most reference books now call this definition 'archaic'. *The Oxford Dictionary of English* refines the meaning by calling it 'the intellectual and practical activity encompassing the systematic study of the structure and behaviour of the physical and natural world through observation and experiment'.[3]

This brings us a little closer to where we need to be for the purposes of this book. Science seeks to discover, observe and understand the principles and laws that govern the natural world. It is not static, but dynamic; not a product, but a process; not an entity, but an enterprise. It is 'work in progress', an honest, open-ended, ongoing, objective, painstaking pursuit of reliable knowledge about our world and everything in it. It addresses an endless stream of questions, using what we now call 'the scientific method' — observation, the formulation of hypotheses that fit the data, the examination of other possibilities, and repeated experiments (that can either succeed or fail). When scientists have jumped through all those hoops they can reasonably claim to have established a scientific theory. Speaking on BBC television, philosopher Danah Zohar said, 'Great science is about asking great questions... Science invites us to investigate, to look further, beyond appearances, to see what lies behind.'[4] Richard Bube, Emeritus Professor of Materials Science and Electrical Engineering at America's Stanford University, adds an important touch: 'Science is a way of knowing *based on human interpretation of publicly obtained data through interaction with the physical world.*'[5] To put all of this more simply, science is the ongoing process of learning things about the natural world. We shall use this as a working definition from now on.

As to the second key word in our title, I have deliberately not asked, 'Has science got rid of *religion?' The Oxford Dictionary of English* defines religion as 'the belief in and worship of a superhuman controlling power, especially a personal God or gods',[6] and the distinguished British scientist Sir John Houghton notes that religion has always been a universal phenomenon: 'There is general evidence that most human beings, from whatever part of the world and from the earliest times, have exhibited a fundamental belief in a divine being or beings, and in some sort of spiritual world.'[7] Religion comes in all shapes and sizes and its claims range from the amusing to the amazing. Animism encourages the worship of spirits said to live in all natural phenomena, from rocks to rivers and from trees to flowers. Pantheism leans in the same direction by saying that God is everything and everything is God. Polytheism points to an unlimited number of gods. The New Age Movement claims that all its members are divine (which presumably means that an extra deity is added to the total whenever a person joins). Religious zealots have indulged in all kinds of bizarre rituals to bind themselves to their beliefs: painting or mutilating their bodies, sacrificing their children, or even burning themselves to death. In the United States alone there are well over 2,600 faith groups, 250 of them newly listed in *The Encyclopaedia of American Religion* since 1999. The Kennedy Worshippers have declared the former U.S. president a deity; All-One-God-Faith is a soap company; and the Embassy of Heaven issues its own vehicle number plates because it considers all earthly govern- ments illegitimate.

The big five

In these days it is fashionable to lump all religions together and to say that they all amount to the same thing. Speaking at a rally held in Yankee Stadium, New York. a few days after the horrific terrorist attacks in the United States on 11 September 2001, television personality Oprah Winfrey told the world that all people pray to the same God. The claim was carefully

crafted to avoid political confrontation, but it was complete
nonsense. As we can easily show, the idea that all religions are
equally valid paths to ultimate spiritual reality falls apart at the
seams as soon as we try to pick it up. Although our modern
world is awash with structured religions and cults — Baha'ism,
Confucianism, Shinto, Sikhism, Zoroastrianism, Hare Krishna,
Mormonism, Jehovah's Witnesses, the Church of Scientology,
Transcendental Meditation, to name just a few — 'religion' to
most people usually means Hinduism, Buddhism, Islam,
Judaism or Christianity. We can make our point by limiting
ourselves to these.

   Hinduism, which dates back at least as far as 3,000 B.C.,
has been called 'a family of religions … fluid and changing'.[8] Its
bewildering assortment of religious and philosophical ideas is
said to accommodate no fewer than thirty-three million gods[9]
and one authority goes so far as to say that Hindus 'can be
pantheists, polytheists, monotheists, agnostics or even atheists'.[10]

   Buddhism is based on the teachings of Siddhartha
Gautama, who was born about 563 B.C. (though his arrival is
said to have been the last of at least 550 reincarnations). Some
modern Mahayana Buddhists worship him, along with many
other gods borrowed from Hinduism, but traditional Buddhism
does not have a personal god.

   Islam is the youngest and second largest of the world's major
religions. Its teachings are enshrined in the Qur'an, made up of
visions said to have been received by Muhammad, who was
born in the Arabian city of Mecca at some time between A.D.
570-580, and statements based on things he said. Like Buddha,
Muhammad made no claim to divinity. Islam's deity is Allah, an
austere and remote figure unaffected by people's actions and
attitudes and 'not personally knowable'.[11]

   Judaism is a worldwide phenomenon that has shown an
amazing ability to adapt itself to pressure and persecution from
secular and religious sources. Its teaching is derived from the
Bible's Old Testament but is centred on the Torah. This consists
of the Mishnah and the Gemara, writings based on the first five

books of the Bible and laying down 613 precepts for living —
though these need not all apply in exceptional circumstances.
Judaism stresses the uniqueness and transcendence of God, but
not his intimate interaction with humankind.

Christianity takes the entire Bible to be 'the living and
enduring word of God'.[12] This reveals God as the sovereign
creator of all reality outside of himself, including time and space:
'... the universe was formed at God's command.'[13] God did not
create because he had to, but because he chose to. Nothing in
creation needs any justification beyond the fact that in his
infinite wisdom God willed it to be, and in his infinite power
brought it into being. God is not merely a cosmic force or
'higher power', but is both personal and eternally self-existent,
'from everlasting to everlasting'.[14] He exists as a Trinity of
distinguishable persons, identified in the Bible as the Father, the
Son and the Holy Spirit.[15] He is perfect in all his ways,[16] un-
changeable[17] and 'abounding in love'.[18]

He is the sole and sovereign ruler over all that he has made:
'His kingdom rules over all.'[19] He sustains the entire created
order and governs the natural world, the spiritual world, international affairs, earthly authorities and the lives of individual
human beings: he 'works out everything in conformity with the
purpose of his will'.[20] Ultimately, the final destiny of every
human being is in his hands and he will 'judge the world with
justice'.[21]

God's relationship with humankind is centred in the fact that
about 2,000 years ago he broke into history in the person of
Jesus Christ, who assumed humanity while retaining his deity.
His virgin birth, perfect life and voluntary death in the place of
others were all hallmarks of his deity, confirmed by his resurrection from the dead,[22] which showed him to be 'the true God',[23]
who promises the forgiveness of sins and eternal life to all who
put their trust in him.[24]

Even on the basis of this sketchy overview, it is perfectly
obvious that all religions are *not* the same. Even an entrenched
atheist like the British philosopher Bertrand Russell noted, 'It is

evident as a matter of logic that, since they disagree, not more than one of them can be true,'[25] while the *Daily Telegraph's* Janet Daley fine-tuned the point: 'You cannot defend all faiths — at least not at the same time — because each has beliefs that render those of the others false.'[26] This is as clear as daylight. Many major world religions, let alone hundreds of smaller ones, make claims that are diametrically opposed to one another when dealing with the existence and nature of God and the possibility of our having a living relationship with him. When this happens it is simply impossible that they can all be right. Nor is there any mileage in the trendy idea that a given religion may be 'true for one person but not for another'. A belief is either true for everybody or nobody, and no compromise is possible. As a modern writer has said, 'To say "All roads lead to God" is as illogical as saying that a bus ride to the shops is much the same as taking a trip to the moon on a space shuttle. The route, mode of transport and destination are all completely different!'[27]

It has been said that all the study of comparative religion does is to make people comparatively religious! Be that as it may, the idea that all religions point in the same direction, or lead to the same destination, is clearly ridiculous. Christianity is based on an extended series of momentous historical events recorded in the Bible, whereas all other faiths, ancient or modern, are built on the subjective moral and ethical teaching of their founders or leaders. The contemporary apologist Joe Boot fleshes out this critical distinction: 'The Bible is not a book of elevated moral philosophy or eloquent prose but is based on objective, historical facts *open to verification*. The Bible does not ask us to accept an ethical teaching simply because it says so. Instead, it calls on us to test its coherence and validity. The Bible is an account of what God has done for us in human history and how he has spoken and acted in our world, which is why we can test the Bible to see whether it is true. All other religions fail the same tests.'[28]

Although some of what is to follow is true of the relationship between science and all religious faiths, I am writing as a committed Christian, convinced intellectually, emotionally and experientially that the entire Bible is 'God-breathed',[29] an inerrant revelation of God's nature and will.

2.
Scientism: the godless god

Now that we have nailed down our definitions, we can tackle the question head-on. Has science, the ongoing, open-ended search for truth in the natural world, got rid of the God revealed in the Bible as the transcendent creator of all reality outside of himself, who controls every atom in the universe, who broke into time and space in the person of Jesus Christ, and to whom each one of us is morally and eternally accountable? Scientists, theologians and philosophers have wrestled with the question *ad infinitum* and have been joined by countless millions of 'ordinary' people who have been fascinated by the issue. At the beginning of his book *The Search for God: Can science help?*, Sir John Houghton identifies four different attitudes that have been adopted when discussing man's quest for truth. The first says that the scientific method is the only valid way, the second that faith is the only way, the third that science and faith overlap, and the fourth that they are mutually exclusive.[1]

We shall touch on the last three of these as we go along, but shall concentrate here on the first, a view for which it is not difficult to find an eloquent spokesman. At the time of writing, Peter Atkins is SmithKline Beecham Fellow and Tutor in Physical Chemistry at Lincoln College, Oxford. He has written college textbooks such as *General Chemistry; Physical Chemistry* (the world's best-seller on the subject); *Inorganic Chemistry; Molecular Quantum Mechanics; Quanta* and *Concepts of*

Physical Chemistry, as well as more broadly aimed volumes such as, *Molecules; The Second Law; Atoms, Electrons and Change* and *The Periodic Kingdom*. We can therefore assume that Atkins is able to speak seriously about science in general and with considerable authority on his particular discipline. Yet he finds his way onto these pages not because of his track record in the world of science, but because he is a passionate and eloquent atheist who claims with dogmatic panache that science has now obliterated God — a view that fits perfectly with his position as an Honorary Associate of the National Secular Society. In the course of a debate at Oxford University in 1998 he said, 'I am on the brink of understanding everything and I commend you to use your brains, because your brains are the most wonderful instruments in the universe, and through your brains you will see that you can do without God. There is no necessity for God because *science can explain everything.*' In an article published in the *Independent* four years later he described religions as 'quaint ways of disguising ignorance, propagating wishful thinking and exercising power over the ignorant and weak', then targeted Christianity in particular, accusing it of propagating 'manifest nonsense that is totally incompatible with our scientific understanding of the world'.[2]

This is rousing language — but it is not science! Instead, it is *scientism,* which uses much of science's terminology, but has few of its virtues. Scientism often trades under the names of materialism, naturalism or reductionism, titles that give clear clues as to where it is coming from. Materialism can be traced as far back as Greek philosophers such as Thales (who lived around 585 B.C.) and Democritus (*c.* 460–370 B.C.). The latter is sometimes called 'the father of materialism' and taught that all reality consisted of nothing but a vast number of self-propelled atoms whirling around in space. In the nineteenth century the German philosopher Ludwig Feuerbach adopted the same line: 'There is nothing beyond nature and man... Any solution that seeks to go beyond the boundaries of nature and man is worthless.'[3] One of his contemporaries who was powerfully influenced by Feuerbach was Karl Marx, whose doctorate at the University of Jena was on the materialism (and atheism) of Democritus and like-minded Greek thinkers. Yet far from being part of science, materialism is a philosophy *about* science. It says that all of reality can be explained without the need to go beyond the material or natural, and that only natural (as opposed to supernatural or spiritual) laws and forces are at work in the world. More concisely put, this says that everything in the world can be reduced to matter and chance.

In his book *The Clockwork Image*,[4] the British physicist and brain scientist Professor Donald MacKay, who was Research Professor of Communications and Neuroscience at the University of Keele, coined the term 'nothing-buttery' to describe this idea. It was a good choice, as materialism claims that everything can be reduced to *nothing but* atoms and molecules and that the only valid explanation for a natural phenomenon is a scientific one. One of the simplest summaries I have come across was given by the hugely popular astronomer, author and pioneer in exobiology, Carl Sagan, whose PBS television series *Cosmos* was seen by some five per cent of the world's population: 'The cosmos is all that is or ever was or ever will be.'[5]

The agenda

As we shall see in a later chapter, modern science can be said to date from the time when scientists who believed in God as the creator of the universe began to lean heavily on the scientific method in investigating natural causes. Scientism has turned the whole process on its head by rejecting God altogether, claiming that only natural causes exist and that they do so independently. The idea has grown dramatically over the last 200 years, so that far from being a minority view left over from less sophisticated times, materialism has a powerful grip on contemporary society, especially in mainstream educational circles.

In his excellent book *Reason in the Balance,* Berkeley law professor Phillip Johnson notes, 'The most influential intellectuals in America and around the world are mostly *naturalists*, who assume that God exists only as an idea in the minds of religious believers. In our greatest universities, naturalism — the doctrine that nature is "all there is" — is the virtually unquestioned assumption that underlies not only natural science but intellectual work of all kinds.'[6] Professor Kirsten Birkett, Director of the Matthias Centre for the Study of Modern Beliefs, agrees and says that materialism 'is now the assumed view in most secular institutions and publications'.[7]

Recent surveys in the United States seem to confirm this. While about 90% of those polled said they believed in God, only about 40% of scientists said so, while among members of the prestigious U.S. National Academy of Sciences (the 'top brass' of the country's scientists) the figure dropped to less than 10%. Just as importantly, it has been suggested that '… the group of scientists most responsible for presenting "science" to the wider community is dominated by people who have explicitly adopted atheism and a materialistic philosophy of life.'[8]

None of this alters the fact that a significant number of world-class scientists reject materialism, but it does help to explain why it has an increasing hold on countless millions of people who have never given it any sustained thought.

As Phillip Johnson explains, it is easy to see that materialism has radical religious implications: 'If naturalism is true, then humankind created God — not the other way around. In that case, rationality requires that we recognize the Creator as the imaginary being he has always been, and that we rely only on things that are real, such as ourselves and the material world of nature.'[9] This is a fundamental factor in materialism and points to the fact that card-carrying materialists have a specific agenda. Professor Stephen Barr, a theoretical-particle physicist at the Bartol Research Institute of the University of Delaware, puts it like this: 'For many, scientific materialism is not a bloodless philosophy but a passionately held ideology… Its adherents see

science as having a mission that goes beyond the mere investigation of nature or the discovery of physical laws. That mission
is to free mankind from superstition in all its forms, and especially in the form of religion.'[10]

Nobody provides a better example of this than Peter Atkins.
After the September 11 terrorist attacks the British government
moved to introduce a law aimed at preventing 'incitement to
religious hatred'. In response, Peter Atkins wrote a letter to *The
Times Higher Education Supplement* in which he railed against
religion as denying the power of the human intellect, encouraging laziness as a mode of argument, being deceitful in offering
benefits in the afterlife, blighting individual freedom and encouraging violence. His two opening sentences revealed the aim
that lay behind the assault: '*This letter is intended to be an
incitement to religious hatred.* I believe it is not yet a crime to
encourage people to despise religion and almost all it stands for,
but as time is running out for freedom of expression, I thought it
appropriate to try and save the world from itself before it is too
late.'[11]

Quoted in the *Independent* twelve years earlier, the British
philosopher — and materialist — Sir Alfred Ayer was even
more passionate (though adopting a strange turn of phrase!):
'My God, my God, I shall die a happy man if I make one
person disbelieve in God.'[12]

This confirms materialism's agenda, which is to free mankind
from all forms of religious belief: firstly, because religion insists
that there is a spiritual world beyond nature; and, secondly,
because in the materialist's eyes religion is irrational, depending
on nothing more than faith at best and superstition at worst,
something that developed during a primitive stage in the
evolution of the human species.

Richard Dawkins, the Charles Simonyi Professor of the
Public Understanding of Science at Oxford University (and
Britain's best-known atheist), makes no bones about this. In a
television interview he expressed his annoyance that some
people 'spend enormous amounts of time learning church

teachings' because 'to me, religion is very largely an enemy of truth'.[13] Elsewhere, he famously attacked religion as 'a virus of the mind'[14] and called religious faith 'stupefied superstition'.[15]

The two British scientists Francis Crick and James Watson, who took the world by storm in 1953 with their discovery of the double-helical structure of DNA, have both attacked religion with similar enthusiasm. Crick said that it was distaste for religion that drove him into science. In 1961, Crick resigned as a Fellow of Churchill College, Cambridge, when it proposed to build a chapel. When Sir Winston Churchill wrote to tell him that only those who wished to do so need enter the chapel, Crick replied that on those grounds the college should build a brothel — and enclosed a cheque for ten guineas towards the cost![16] Watson called religious explanations 'myths from the past' and told the *Daily Telegraph*, 'Every time you understand something, religion becomes less likely.'[17]

These men are heavy hitters, so have to be reckoned with in their particular fields of scientific expertise, but none of them is an authority on the subject of religion, and I am not aware that any one of them has produced a shred of evidence to back up their extravagant claims.

As far as the Christian faith is concerned, attacking it as mere superstition is misplaced. Stephen Barr points out that the Bible countered this criticism long before the advent of modern science: 'The Book of Genesis was itself in large part intended, scholars tell us, as a polemic against pagan superstition. For example, whereas the sun and moon were the objects of worship in pagan religion, the Book of Genesis taught that they were nothing but lamps set in the heavens to give light to day and night: not gods, but mere things, creatures of the one true God. Nor were animals and the forces of nature to be bowed down to by man as in pagan religion; rather man, as a rational being made in the image of God, was to exercise dominion over them.'[18]

What we need to grasp here (with Crick's confession as a good illustration) is that materialists are driven, not by the kind

of facts they demand in their science, but by their world-view.
Wherever the evidence seems to point, they refuse to go
beyond physics to metaphysics.

It would be difficult for anyone to be more up-front about
this than Professor Richard Lewontin, geneticist, biologist and
social commentator at Harvard University: 'Our willingness to
accept scientific claims that are against common sense is the key
to an understanding of the real struggle between science and
the supernatural. We take the side of science *in spite* of the
patent absurdities of some of its constructs, *in spite* of its failure
to fulfil many of its extravagant promises of health and life, *in
spite* of the tolerance of the scientific community for just-so
stories, *because we have a prior commitment to materialism.* It
is not that the methods and institutions of science somehow
compel us to accept a material explanation of the phenomenal
world, but, on the contrary, that we are forced by our *a priori*
adherence to material causes to create an apparatus of investigation and a set of concepts that produce material explanations,
no matter how counter-intuitive, no matter how mystifying to
the uninitiated. Moreover that materialism is absolute for *we
cannot allow a Divine foot in the door.*'[19]

This lets a huge cat out of scientism's bag! In layman's
language, Lewontin is saying that regardless of how illogical,
unsatisfying or implausible certain materialistic hypotheses and
constructs seem to be, they have to be accepted *simply because
they are materialistic.* This hardly qualifies as honest science
and it seems strange that hard-core materialists appear to miss
this point. Richard Dawkins says that if he were asked for a
single phrase to characterize his role as Professor of the Public
Understanding of Science he would choose 'Advocate for
Disinterested Truth'[20] — yet he is passionately committed to a
materialism that will not allow any other claim to have a
hearing!

This kind of dogmatism hardly does materialism a favour,
because as Kirsten Birkett points out, 'Whether or not naturalism is true, it cannot be proved true by the very activity that

pragmatically chooses not to discuss the alternative. The scientific method (as practised by the scientific community) will never "discover" supernatural causes, since it does not look for them and by definition cannot accept them.'[21]

Stephen Barr underlines the importance of this as we try to answer the question being posed in this book: 'What many take to be a conflict between religion and science is really something else. It is a conflict between religion and materialism. Material-ism regards itself as scientific, and indeed is often called "scien-tific materialism", even by its opponents, but *it has no legitimate claim to be part of science.*'[22]

Questions…[23]

In his book *Blind Alley Beliefs*, the British philosopher David Cook imagines what would happen if all the national news-papers came out with the headline, 'Materialism is true', and ran a series of articles to back up the claim. He then asks how that might affect the population at large. If we became con-vinced that the newspapers were right and that even our thinking and feelings could be traced to nothing but matter, what difference would it make to the way we lived? Cook goes on: 'After the shock and novelty had worn off, life would be the same… There is something extremely odd about a view which is true and correct, but does not make any difference at all. What kind of view is it that is true, but does not in fact affect *anything* we do? It seems a strangely remote kind of truth.'[24]

Cook is right, in that much of modern society is saturated with materialism, which has become the determining influence on people's ethics, lifestyle and relationships. Yet if materialism is true it raises a raft of questions to which it can produce no answers:

- If there is no absolute beyond the existence of matter, how can there be a transcendent truth that tells us this is the case?
- If human beings are nothing more than accidental items in a universal mass of matter — Atkins says that humankind is 'just a bit of slime on a planet'[25] — how can a person have individual value or personal worth?
- If matter is all there is, what possible meaning can we give to concepts such as good, evil, morality, justice, truth, love, beauty, desire, or hope?
- How does the materialist explain creativity in the worlds of music, drama, art — or science, for that matter?
- If human beings are purely material, where can we find a source for imagination or belief?
- If a human being is just a mass of matter, how or why does he or she remember the past, evaluate the present and anticipate the future?

These are no more than examples of the questions materialism has to face because it refuses to recognize an important distinction — namely, that while science is a tool which man can use with amazing effectiveness in many areas, there are many other areas beyond its reach. We shall develop this in the next chapter, but we should no more expect science to answer every question we can ask than we should use a pea-shooter to launch a space probe, or a pickaxe to do brain surgery.

The distinguished Brazilian-born zoologist Peter Medawar, who became Director of London's National Institute for Medical Research, made the point like this: 'There is no quicker way for a scientist to bring discredit upon himself and upon his profession than roundly to declare — particularly when no declaration of any kind is called for — that science knows or soon will know the answers to all questions worth asking, and that questions which do not admit a scientific answer are in some way "nonquestions" or "pseudoquestions" that only simpletons ask and only the gullible profess to be able to answer.'[26] Scientism suggests that the scientific method is the only way to find answers but, as Donald MacKay humorously showed, this is clearly not the case: 'The man who in the name of intellectual integrity tries to win a wife in the way in which he'd tackle a problem in thermodynamics has the wrong idea of what intellectual integrity means, and is very likely to remain a bachelor.'[27]

Men or machines?

The questions we have posed so far are more than awkward for materialists, but these are not the only ones they have to face. This is because materialism goes hand in glove with determinism, which says that everything we do is conditioned by heredity and environment. The link is obvious: if there is no God, or other transcendent reality, all we have is a closed, mechanistic universe, with humankind as one of its 'working parts'. Nobody seriously denies that some chemical, psychological and sociological factors affect the way people think and act, but this falls a long way short of determinism, which says that *all* our decisions are the inevitable result of materialistic factors over which we have no control.

As human beings, we are not only aware of sensations, we reflect on them. We engage in complex reasoning and lateral thinking; we evaluate data, develop ideas, exercise imagination and make decisions. Yet Peter Atkins insists that '... at the deepest level, decisions are adjustments of the dispositions in the molecules inside large numbers of cells in the brain.'[28] Richard Dawkins takes the same line and argues that love is 'a product of highly complicated equipment of some sort, nervous equipment or computing equipment of some sort'.[29] But is this an adequate explanation of the powerful emotions and life-changing experiences we associate with the word 'love'? The experimental psychologist Steven Pinker endorses Atkins and

Dawkins and bluntly claims, 'Nothing in the mind exists except as neural activity.'[30] Materialists lean heavily on this kind of thinking, but astrophysicist Rodney Holder easily points out its radical and fatal flaw: 'If we are nothing but atoms and molecules organized in a particular way through the chance processes of evolution, then love, beauty, good and evil, free will, reason itself — indeed all that makes us human and raises us above the rest of the created order — lose their objectivity. Why should I love my neighbour, or go out of my way to help him? Rather, why should I not get everything I can for myself, trampling on whoever gets in my way?'[31]

Materialistic determinism cannot possibly be squared with moral, responsible human living. The difference between human beings and machines is not just relative, but absolute. In the course of his 1967 Reith Lectures, the English anthropologist scholar Sir Edmund Leach claimed, 'There is no sharp break between what is human and what is mechanical,' but this is nonsensical. If we are nothing but what someone has called 'computers made of meat' we should presumably apply the same moral concepts in our dealings with computers as we do in our dealings with one another. Alternatively, as the mathematician and physicist Roger Penrose argues, if we are nothing but computers, programmed in a certain way, then our reason, emotions, love and aesthetic feelings are all meaningless.[32] The simple fact is that determinism is not liveable. What is more, the distinguished philosopher of science Sir Karl Popper maintains that if it were true *it could not even be argued*, since any argument made in its defence would itself presumably have been predetermined, along with any arguments against it![33]

True science is honest, open-ended, reasonable and humble. Scientism is exactly the opposite. It is pseudo-science, and not only arrogant, irrational and illogical, but cruel, robbing us of any basis for dignity, meaning, purpose or hope. As Peter Atkins openly admits in *Creation Revisited*, 'Everything is driven by motiveless, purposeless decay.'[34]

Unbelieving believers

Scientism is not true science, but a belief system superimposed on an activity. In the course of a visit to South Africa a few years ago, I was invited to take part in a radio programme produced in Cape Town. For days beforehand the programme was trailed as 'Believer versus Unbeliever'. The one-hour show began with the presenter (an atheist) introducing me as the believer and himself as the unbeliever, but in my opening comments I questioned the whole premise of the programme and insisted that he, too, was a believer. He strongly challenged this, but I pointed out, 'I gladly admit that I am a believer — I believe in the existence of God. But you are a believer too — you believe in the non-existence of God. What I would like you to share with the listeners is the evidence on which you base your faith in God's non-existence.' He was completely at a loss what to say. This was hardly surprising, because one would need to possess all the evidence available in the universe before one could be sure that there is none pointing to God's existence.

People can choose *what* to believe, but not *whether* to believe, as faith is built into the whole business of being human. As author Martin Robinson points out, 'Those who characterize themselves as "unbelievers" do not believe in nothing. On the contrary, they often have a very definite set of beliefs, which may be held just as passionately as so-called "believers" hold to the tenets of their faith.'[35] We shall pursue this in a later chapter, but the point needs to be made here because it holes scientism below the waterline. Science makes much of the verification principle, which says that in order to be accepted as true a theory must be capable of verification or falsification. But if this is the case, how can we prove scientifically that the only reality is that which can be proved scientifically? Scientism says, 'What you see is what you get' — *but how can we know this?* When scientism says that only what can be known and proved by science is rational and true it is being *irrational*, because the claim itself cannot be proved scientifically! To say that 'Seeing is believing' is hardly good enough. For the materialist to claim that nothing else is possible, he needs more backing than the statement that there is nothing else that he can see. As someone has said, 'What could be more inconsistent than to limit one's system to observable phenomena, and then make pronouncements about the non-observable?' J. P. Moreland rightly says, 'One cannot turn to science to justify science any more than one can pull oneself up by [one's] own bootstraps.'[36] For scientism to say that God does not exist it has to abandon the rules by which it operates when making its own claims.

The British journalist Bryan Appleyard calls scientism 'dangerously seductive propaganda',[37] but the Bible goes further than that. All truth ultimately has its source in God, who created all reality outside of himself and sustains all that he created. In the person of his Son, Jesus Christ, he told Pontius Pilate, 'Everyone on the side of truth listens to me.'[38] To elevate any purely human idea to the same level is nothing less than idolatry.

3.
Reality check: science and its limits

If we accept that scientific investigation is being carried out whenever human beings try to find out how the world works, it is impossible for us to know when 'science' began, but it is usually accepted that in its modern form it dates from about the early part of the seventeenth century. The breakthrough was led by the remarkable English courtier, politician, philosopher and scientist Sir Francis Bacon. Born in 1561, he became in turn a barrister, a solicitor, a Member of Parliament, a baron, a viscount, King's Counsel, Solicitor General, Attorney General, Privy Councillor and Lord Chancellor. In his famous *Novum Organum*, first published in 1620, he put forward a new idea which became known as the inductive method, stressing the importance of observation and experiment. Bacon saw himself as the inventor of a method of kindling a light in nature 'that would eventually disclose and bring to light all that is most hidden and secret in the universe'. These are wildly extravagant claims, but Bacon's influence is reflected in the many titles he has been given, among them 'The Secretary of Nature', 'the father of inductive reasoning' and 'the prophet of modern science'.[1] (As an interesting footnote, his restless search for truth led indirectly to his death. While driving near Highgate in 1626 he decided to experiment with the effect of cold on the decay of meat. While stuffing a fowl with snow he caught a cold which developed into fatal bronchitis.)

The torch that Bacon and others lit has been blazing ever since and nobody can seriously deny that science and its daughter, technology, are revolutionizing our lives in ways that would have been beyond belief a hundred years ago. In 1899, Charles H. Duell, a Commissioner of the US Office of Patents, claimed, 'Everything that can be invented has been invented.' In 1943 IBM's Chairman Thomas Watson said, 'I think there is a world market for maybe five computers'! In 1949 an article in *Popular Scientist* suggested that computers might eventually weigh as little as 1.5 tons! There is said to be more digital technology in today's average mobile telephone than there was on the spacecraft that in 1969 put the first man on the moon.

Science and technology are filling our lives with a constant flow of gadgets, devices and equipment aimed at making our lives longer, fuller, easier and more enjoyable. Had I lived in the seventeenth century I would have played golf with a more-or-less round leather pouch stuffed with a hatful of boiled feathers. The ball I use today has an intertwined molecular construction combining zinc diacrylate and high density rubber. In heavy rain, a seventeenth-century golfer would have got soaking wet (and possibly caught fatal pneumonia). Today, I am protected by a Teflon-coated rain suit with a hydrophilic laminate outer layer, a capillary-style membrane and a technical mesh drop-line (whatever that means!), the whole technological triumph weighing less than 700 grams.

Bryan Appleyard writes, 'This unarguable and spectacular effectiveness is the ace up science's sleeve... You are dissatis-fied with the quality and convenience of music in your home? Here is a compact disc player. You wish to avoid smallpox? Here is an injection. You wish to go to the moon? Here is a rocket. You are hungry? Here is how to grow more food. You are too fat? Here is how to lose weight. You feel bad? Here is a pill, feel better. No problem, says science.'[2]

There is a pointer here to the reason that many people think science and religion have become divorced. As we shall see in a later chapter, the scientific method was built on a God-centred view of nature, but influential movers and shakers began to pull away from this idea and to suggest that God might be superfluous. Today, increased knowledge of the physical universe and phenomenal achievements in technology have tended to accelerate the movement. Who needs God when we can transplant human organs, manipulate genes and produce an endless conveyor belt of 'wonder drugs' to control or eliminate diseases that proved fatal a few years ago? In 1941 the British biologist Sir Julian Huxley wrote, 'Natural science has pushed God into an ever greater remoteness, until his function as ruler and dictator disappears,'[3] adding elsewhere, 'God is simply fading away.'[4] In today's world, science 'has come to be seen as a sacred cow which, if appropriately fed, will continue to yield tangible benefits for the good of all'.[5] Dyed-in-the-wool materialists like Sir Edmund Leach go even further: 'Men have become like gods. Isn't it about time we understood our divinity? Science offers us total mastery over our environment and our destiny.'[6]

Descriptions, corrections, dissension

There are at least four reasons why Leach is wrong.

1. The scientific description of something is not the only one

If you were visiting me and I were to say, 'I am going to infuse *Camellia sinensis* leaves in a liquid compound of oxygen and hydrogen,' you might wonder what I meant, but this is a scientific way of stating, 'I am going to make the tea.' If I were to say to my wife, 'Let us juxtapose our orbicular muscles and have a reciprocal transmission of carbon dioxide and microbes,' I would expect a puzzled frown, but if I made the same

suggestion in non-scientific language — 'I would like to kiss
you' — I would hope to get a more encouraging response! If
you invited me to watch somebody rubbing the entrails of a
dead sheep with the hairs of a dead horse you would meet with
a decidedly cool reception, but if you were to phrase the same
invitation differently and ask me to join you in listening to a
violin solo I might want to check my diary.[7] By the same token,
to say that a piano concerto is nothing more than black blobs
and lines on sheets of paper is hardly to tell the whole story!

2. Scientific statements are not set in concrete

The history of science has numerous examples of scientific
'facts' that have later been abandoned in the light of subsequent
discoveries. Here are ten examples to make the point:

- The second-century Egyptian astronomer and geographer Claudius Ptolemy seems to have convinced everybody that all the heavenly bodies in the universe revolved
  around the earth, and it was not until the sixteenth century that the Polish astronomer Nicolaus Copernicus
  proved him wrong.
- In the seventeenth century the universally acclaimed
  scientist Sir Isaac Newton defined the laws of motion and
  universal gravitation, but scientists have subsequently un-
  covered areas where Newton's laws do not apply.
- In 1760 the Scottish chemist Joseph Black said that
  heat was some kind of extra substance (he called it cal-
  oric) that was added to a hot object and taken away from
  a cold one. This theory was widely accepted, but would
  be laughed out of court today with our knowledge of the
  motions and vibrations of atoms and molecules.
- It was once a scientific 'fact' that a substance called
  'ether' filled all space and carried the 'pulling power' between planets, but experiments in 1887 by the American

physicist Albert Michelson and his colleague Edward
Morley led to the 'ether' idea being abandoned and pre-
pared the way for the general theory of relativity.

• It was once thought that light consisted of a stream of
particles moving through space, but in the nineteenth
century scientists said that this was not the case and that
light should be thought of in terms of waves. Later scientists decided that light had both wave-like and particle-like
characteristics, depending on the experiment involved.

• Medicine used to be based on four 'humours' which
had to be in balance to ensure good health, but no serious physician believes this now.

• When the Hubble Space Telescope made a startling
new discovery a few years ago, a leading scientist told the
press, 'We will have to rewrite the laws of physics.' What
he meant was not that the physical world had changed,
but that scientists would have to change their theories
about it.

• When the British scientist Richard Roberts and his
American colleague Phillip Sharp, co-winners of the 1993
Nobel prize for medicine, revolutionized basic research in
biology by finding that gene sequences are interrupted by
small inserts of DNA called introns, Roberts told the *Daily
Telegraph*, 'It was one of those discoveries where dogma
is overturned.'[8]

• At a conference of the American Association for the
Advancement of Science held in 2002, a leading speaker
said, 'We are very close to a new view of reality. The way
we think about things is about to change.'[9]

• A final illustration is especially relevant to our subject.
In 1861 the French Academy of Sciences, founded 200
years earlier, just as modern science was taking off, published a booklet listing fifty-one scientific 'facts' allegedly
showing that the Bible could not be trusted, but today *not
one* of those 'facts' has any scientific endorsement.

These examples are sufficient to show that true science is always in a state of self-correcting flux. As Carl Sagan put it, 'The history of science is full of cases where previously accepted theories and hypotheses have been overthrown to be replaced by new ideas which more adequately explain the data.'[10] This is why Professor Steve Jones, Professor of Genetics at the University of London, can say, 'Science is the art of the uncertain.'[11] Karl Popper formally underlined this: 'The old scientific idea of *episteme* — of absolutely demonstrable knowledge — has proved an idol. The demand for scientific objectivity makes it inevitable that *every scientific statement must remain tentative for ever.*'[12] Elsewhere he has an excellent illustration to make the point that scientific statements can never be assumed to be absolute: 'The bold structure of its theories rises, as it were, above a swamp. It is like a building erected on piles. The piles are driven down from above, into the swamp, *but not down to any natural or given base*; and when we cease our attempts to drive our piles into deeper layers, *it is not because we have reached firm ground.* We simply stop when we are satisfied that they are firm enough to carry the structure, at least for the time being.'[13]

Even if we find we can use it to our advantage, the best we can do about scientific knowledge is to regard it as provisional. There is no textbook that contains all scientific truth on every subject, and against which we can check every scientific theory. As Del Ratzsch, Professor of Philosophy at Calvin College, Michigan, puts it, 'The Nobel prize committee does not have an answer book against which to check proposed theories.'[14] Science is an ongoing process of learning in which from time to time things once said to be true are found to be false. A cartoon in *New Scientist* makes the point well. Responding to a teacher's statement, a student asks, 'Is that the answer?' 'Yes', the teacher replies. Obviously baffled, the student protests, 'But you told us the opposite yesterday!' 'Jennifer', the teacher counters, 'That was yesterday — we must remember that science is making tremendous strides'! In true science the latest word is not the last word!

3. Scientific statements about a given subject are often contradictory or imprecise

Cosmologists are constantly at loggerheads with one another over whether the universe had a time-related beginning and whether it will end in a 'Big Crunch' or a 'Big Bounce'. Some scientists believe in general relativity; others in spatial particle theory. There is great disagreement over the exact nature of electrons and other subatomic particles. In 1999 a *Sunday Telegraph* review of a book on evolution concluded, 'Modern Darwinian evolutionists are among the bitterest of squabblers,'[15] while the Cambridge biochemist Malcolm Dixon makes the important point that '... there are more disagreements and apparent contradictions within science itself than there are between science and religion.'[16]

Nor can any one branch of science give us a full or strictly accurate picture, as a classic modern fable illustrates. The story goes that a social scientist, a biologist and a physicist went on a hiking holiday to Scotland. Seeing a sheep on a hillside, the social scientist called out, 'Look, the sheep in Scotland are black.' The biologist replied, 'No, you are jumping to conclusions. What you mean is, "In Scotland some sheep are black."' 'Not at all', the physicist protested, 'All we can say from what we have seen is that in Scotland there is at least one sheep, at least one side of which is black'!

4. Vast swathes of knowledge are beyond the reach of science

Speaking on BBC television in 1999, Richard Dawkins claimed, 'I think science really has fulfilled the need that religion did in the past, of explaining things, explaining why we are here, what is the origin of life, where did the world come from, what life is all about,'[17] while later that year he told the *Daily Telegraph Science Extra*, 'Religion is no longer a serious candidate in the field of explanation. It is completely superseded by science.'[18] Yet these fanfares are out of tune with accepted facts, beginning with those relating to the existence and nature of the universe.

Square one

Science is unable to tell us why the universe came into being

In some ancient cultures it was believed that Earth sat fixed in the centre of a static and eternal arrangement of heavenly bodies, with others spread evenly throughout an infinite universe. In the next chapter we shall look at one successful challenge to this idea. Another came in 1915 when the German-born physicist Albert Einstein published his general theory of relativity, which unexpectedly predicted that cosmic space expands. In 1929 the American astronomer Edwin Hubble discovered the expansion of the universe experimentally, while later work by other scientists took this a significant step further, arguing that, if the universe was expanding, at some point in the past all its matter must have been packed closely together into an infinitesimally small point called a 'singularity'. This idea produced the first version of what is now universally known as the 'Big Bang theory', which says that the universe had a definite starting-point — now usually put at around fifteen billion years ago.

The theory has gained such momentum that in a 1995 *Daily Telegraph* poll nearly forty per cent of those interviewed said they believed in a Big Bang 'that produced the raw material of today's universe'.[19] However, in an article accompanying the result of the poll, Steve Jones reminded readers that Big Bang was 'just a theory' and added, 'It might be right, but scientists bicker about it all the time… It might be that the Big Bang will turn out to be a small flop.'[20] Be that as it may, it leaves some much more interesting questions unanswered: Where did the original 'singularity' come from? What do we mean by 'original'? How did it get its energy? When did time begin? What came before 'time zero'? For a modern physicist to tell us, 'Our universe is simply one of those things which happen from time to time,'[21] leaves us none the wiser.

The universally accepted First and Second Laws of Thermodynamics say that the cosmos could not have been self-generated. There has to have been a moment when energy, matter, time and space came into existence. If an eternal, infinite, transcendent and omnipotent God is ruled out, where can science turn to explain the origin of these, when it cannot go any further back than the moment at which the laws on which it leans began to operate? Edgar Andrews pinpoints the problem: 'No matter how close to the instant of origin one may be able to press the scientific model of the cosmos, it remains impossible for such an explanation to be applied at or before the time zero point. Thus it follows that *science, even at its most speculative, must stop short of offering any explanation or even description of the actual event of origin.*'[22]

Hard-core materialists use all kinds of ideas to skate around this. Peter Atkins latches on to what has become known as the quantum fluctuation hypothesis, in which, to quote him in *Creation Revisited*, 'space-time generates its own dust in the process of its own assembly'.[23] Whatever Atkins had in mind, an article in *New Scientist* neatly exposes the weakness of the whole idea: 'First there was nothing, then there is something ... a quantum flutter, a tremor of uncertainty ... and before you know it they have pulled a hundred billion galaxies out of their quantum hats.'[24]

Even those who profess to understand quantum mechanics reach a point at which the laws of physics break down and they are faced with the need to explain where energy and matter came from in the first place, why a Big Bang should ever have happened — and why there should be something rather than nothing. As Michael Poole, lecturer in science education at

King's College London, points out, this leads them into areas beyond the reach of science: 'As soon as scientists begin to ask why there is a Universe to study, or why nature operates in a regular, uniform way, or whether or not there is a mind beyond the laws they observe, they are looking for different types of explanations from a scientific one.'[25] In *Black Holes and Baby Universes,* the British cosmologist Stephen Hawking, Lucasian Professor of Mathematics at Cambridge University, notes, 'Although science may solve the problem of how the universe began, it cannot answer the question: why does the universe bother to exist? I don't know the answer to that.'[26]

Science is unable to explain why there are scientific or natural laws, or why they are so consistent and dependable

Science works because scientists assume the validity, consistency and dependability of the laws of physics, yet there is no scientific explanation of *why* these laws exist, where they come from, or why they operate as they do. Keith Ward, Regius Professor of Divinity at Oxford University, uses an amusing illustration to make the point: 'Suppose the basic laws of physics popped into existence for no reason at all. One day they did not exist. The next day, there they were, governing the behaviour of electrons and atoms. Now if anything at all might pop into existence for no reason, there is actually no way of assessing the probability of laws of physics doing so. One day, there might be nothing. The next day, there might be a very large carrot. Nothing else in existence whatsoever, but there, all alone and larger than life, a huge carrot. If anything is possible, that certainly is. The day after that, the carrot might disappear and be replaced by a purple spotted gorilla. Why not? We are in a universe, or a non-universe, where anything or nothing might happen, for no reason. Why does this seem odd, or even ridiculous, whereas the thought that some law of physics might just pop into existence does not? Logically, they are exactly on a par.'[27]

There is more to the world than physics can ever explain or express, and science has no idea how energy came to be distributed in such a way that our universe is cosmos, not chaos. Edgar Andrews puts it well: 'If we ask science why the laws are such as they are, and not otherwise, if we ask why the law of gravity is an inverse square law with respect to distance, science can do nothing but shrug its mathematical shoulders and reply, "That question lies outside my terms of reference."'[28] When Peter Atkins tells us that, for all its staggering immensity, diversity and interlocking order, the entire universe is 'an elaborate and engaging rearrangement of nothing',[29] he is hardly making a helpful contribution to the subject.

Science cannot explain why the universe is so amazingly fine-tuned to support intelligent life on our planet

For Earth to function as it does in sustaining life, there needs to be an extremely complex and exact arrangement of terrestrial and extra-terrestrial elements. To give some of the best-known examples, the size of Earth, its rotational speed, the tilt of its axis relative to the plane of its orbit, its distance from the sun and its land/water ratio all have to be correct. We need light, but not too much ultra-violet; heat, but not too much. We need the earth's magnetic field to shield us from cosmic rays, atmosphere over our heads to shield us from meteorites and a screen of rock under our feet to prevent us from being incinerated. The Oxford scholar J. L. Mackie, one of the twentieth century's most influential atheists, admitted in his book *The Miracle of Theism*, 'It is … surprising that the elements of this unique set-up are just right for life when they might easily have been wrong.'[30]

He is hardly exaggerating. In recent years science has assembled a complex mass of evidence to support the so-called 'anthropic principle', which says that the universe is fine-tuned to support intelligent life on our planet. This includes the relationship between the relative strengths of the four funda-mental forces of nature (gravity, electromagnetism, the strong nuclear force and the weak nuclear force), the mass ratio of the proton and the neutron, two of the three subatomic particles that form the atom (the proton is 1,836 times more massive than the electron) and the slight excess of matter over antimatter. It has been said that had the excess of matter over antimatter been different by about one particle per ten billion our life-sustaining world would never have come into being.[31] Had there been equal amounts there would have been 'a vast annihilation event' leaving 'only very few particles of matter and antimatter in scattered, isolated remnants'.[32] In addition, the way in which the critical density of the universe affects the gravitational attraction between cosmic structures had to be meticulously accurate. Even accepting today's most popular theory about origins, Stephen Hawking nevertheless says, 'If the rate of expansion one second after the Big Bang had been smaller *by even one part in a hundred thousand million million*, the universe would have recollapsed before it ever reached its present size.'[33] The balance between the effects of expansion and contraction is so precise that Paul Davies, Professor of Natural Philosophy in the Australian Centre for Astrobiology at Macquarie University, Sydney, likens it to aiming at a target an inch wide on the other side of the observable universe and hitting the mark.[34]

I have gone into more detail about fine-tuning and related matters elsewhere,[35] but one more example will round out this section. Carbon and oxygen are essential for life, yet the structure of the carbon atom depends on such narrow tolerances that even the slightest deviation would have made life impossible. Commenting on the precise energy levels required, Astronomer Royal Sir Martin Rees and science writer John Gribbin concluded, 'This combination of coincidences, just right for resonance in carbon-12, just wrong in oxygen-16, is indeed remarkable. *There is no better evidence to support the argument that the universe has been designed for our benefit — tailor-made for man.*'[36] Rees and Gribbin both reject the idea of a personal Creator, but when the world-renowned astronomer

Sir Fred Hoyle grasped the implications of what they found he confessed, 'Nothing has shaken my atheism as much as this discovery.'[37] Stephen Hawking goes even further and says, 'It would be very difficult to explain why the universe should have begun in just this way, *except as the act of a God who intended to create beings just like us.*'[38]

Life and living

Science cannot explain why as human beings we are persons and not merely objects

Science can tell us amazing things about our physical structure. Our bodies have over 100 joints, 200 bones and 600 muscles, all working together in perfect harmony; our hands, powerful enough to wield a sledgehammer yet delicate enough to conduct microsurgery, have over 652,000 nerve endings; our eyes, with 130 million receptor cells packed into their tiny retinas, can handle over 500,000 messages simultaneously; our hearts beat 40,000,000 times a year, processing blood through 80,000 miles of blood vessels; our brains, though accounting for only about two per cent of our body weight, have 100 billion neurones, each with up to 100,000 connections to the rest of the brain's network. What is more, the whole human package comes shrink-wrapped in three layers of flexible waterproofing, complete with its own inbuilt air-conditioning system.

These are amazing statistics, yet they give us no explanation as to why we are more than physical phenomena. In February 2001 the international Human Genome Project published its long-awaited report spelling out the three billion letters that make up the human genome. The British physician James Le Fanu told the *Sunday Telegraph* that this 'impressive achieve-ment' was also 'devastating news for science, and in particular for those who, for the past 20 years, have regularly promised us that once the genome is cracked, all that is currently obscure will be made clear'.[39] After pointing out the extent of the information shortfall, he went on, 'The holy grail, the dream that science would soon tell us something significant about what it means to be human, has slipped through our hands — and we are no wiser than before. *The human genome ... can tell us absolutely nothing about the really important things in life.*'[40]

The American physicist and Nobel laureate Stephen Weinberg says that human life is 'a more-or-less farcical outcome of a chain of accidents';[41] Richard Dawkins calls us 'robot vehicles';[42] and Fred Hoyle claims that we are 'no more than ingenious machines that have evolved as strange by-products in an odd corner of the universe'[43] — yet none of these atheistic assertions can explain our *humanity:* our self-consciousness, our ability to remember the past, evaluate the present and contemplate the future, our sense of dignity and worth, and our innate aesthetic appreciation. Vaclav Havel, President of the Czech Republic, rightly says that values like these 'make sense only in the perspective of the infinite and the eternal'.[44] Even an entrenched evolutionist like Michael Ruse, Professor of Philosophy and Zoology at Florida State University, admits, 'Nothing even yet scratches at an explanation of how a transformed ape could produce the magnificence of Beethoven's *Choral Symphony.*'[45] The distinguished twentieth-century thinker Francis Schaeffer painted the wider picture: 'No one has presented an idea, let alone demonstrated it to be feasible, to explain how the impersonal beginning, plus time, plus chance, can give *personality.* We are distracted by a flourish of endless words, and lo, personality has appeared out of the hat.'[46]

Science can tell us nothing about why the mind exists and functions as it does

As we saw in the previous chapter, Peter Atkins called human brains 'the most wonderful instruments in the universe'. Elsewhere he claimed that, at the deepest level, '... decisions are adjustments of the dispositions of the molecules inside large numbers of cells within the brain.'[47] But to dismiss the thinking process in this way is sheer 'nothing-buttery' and gives rise to a host of tremendously important questions. If the brain was programmed by chance, how do we know that it will come up with the truth more often than randomly generated letters will produce meaningful ideas? If human thinking is nothing but complex chemistry, nerve impulses and the firing of synapses, how can we ever say that any given thought — even the thought that this is the case — is rational or true? If what we treat as rational thinking is nothing but 'molecular adjustment', how can we expect it to produce any premise, theory or conclusion on which we can rely? How can we get rationality from non-rational nature? Would we trust a computer print-out if we knew that the instructions in the machine had been programmed by random, non-rational forces? How can we explain our openness to truth? Euan Squires, one-time Professor of Applied Mathematics at the University of Durham, notes, 'It does not seem to be possible to define consciousness in any meaningful way or to describe it in terms of other things.'[48] As the British author G. K. Chesterton put it, '[The materialist] cannot explain why anything should go right, even observation and deduction, why good logic should not be as misleading as bad logic, if they are both movements in the brain of a bewildered ape.'[49] In *Possible Worlds*, published in 1945, the British geneticist (and atheist) J. B. S. Haldane developed this even further: 'If my mental processes are determined wholly by the motions in my brain, I have no reason to suppose that my beliefs are true ... and hence I have no reason for supposing my brain to be composed of atoms.'[50]

Science rightly leans heavily on rational thinking, but to say with Francis Crick that 'our minds can be explained by the interaction of nerve cells and molecules'[51] gets us no further. The Oxford biochemist and Templeton Prize winner Arthur Peacocke, Warden Emeritus at the Society of Ordained Scientists, gives us the simple truth of the matter: 'Science can investigate all the physical aspects of the brain, but there is still something about the mind — and therefore about who you really are — *that it cannot get at.*'[52] The German-born British theoretical physicist Sir Rudolf Peierls, who contributed to the early theory of the neutron-proton system, clinches the point: 'The premise that you can describe in terms of physics the whole function of a human being ... including its knowledge and its consciousness, is untenable. *There is still something missing.*'[53]

Science can add nothing to the inner quality of life

We have already seen some of the many ways in which science and technology can radically affect our lives in terms of things like health, comfort and communication, but these leave the inner qualities of life itself untouched. In 1991 the International Council of Scientific Unions held a conference in Vienna to discuss the likely needs for science and technology in the twenty-first century. Sir John Houghton later assessed the results of a session on the theme 'Quality of Life': 'Although we could largely agree on those factors which ideally make up quality of life, as scientists we could say virtually nothing (and there was considerable debate on the issue) about how to achieve it in practice. In particular, how could we overcome the inherent selfishness, greed and other undesirable characteristics shown by human beings? The problems can be described by science, as can the factors which may exacerbate them, *but science cannot solve them.*'[54]

Science cannot define or explain ethical principles

Recent years have seen great advances in socio-biology, behavioural science and related subjects, yet science has been unable to explain the principles involved in human behaviour. It can say nothing about love, justice, freedom, beauty, goodness, joy or peace. Every sane person acknowledges the existence and authority of the conscience; as long ago as the first century

B.C. the Roman author Publilius Syrus wrote, 'Even where there is no law, there is conscience.'[55] Yet science cannot explain what it is, or why it operates as it does. The *Daily Telegraph* reported that while Richard Dawkins claimed to have 'an ordinary citizen's view of goodness ... all the right emotions against injustice' and 'a strongly developed sense of good', he conceded that '... as a biologist I haven't a very well worked-out story where that comes from.'[56] He went on to suggest that 'good' was 'just something that emerged', but this hardly qualifies as an explanation. Nor does the claim by two other modern scientists that '... ethics, as we understand it, is an illusion fobbed off on us by our genes.'[57] It might be argued that evolution could promote certain instincts, but this falls a long way short of explaining a consistent moral order.

It is impossible to jump from atoms to ethics and from molecules to morality. If we are merely genetically programmed machines, where can we find a consistent basis for moral values? William Provine, one-time Professor of Biological Sciences at Cornell University, who told the 1999 Annual Conference of American Atheists that 'giving up the idea of God is great for a rational mind', made no bones about our position once God is ruled out: 'No inherent moral or ethical laws exist, nor are there any absolute guiding principles for human society. The universe cares nothing for us and we have no ultimate meaning in life.'[58] This is a recipe for moral and social chaos, and science is unable to lift a finger to help us. It offers no moral guidance or values to govern our lives; Karl Popper openly states that '... science cannot make any pronouncement about ethical principles.'[59] Science cannot even tell us how to distinguish between right and wrong, nor why we should choose one rather than the other. J. B. S. Haldane said bluntly, 'Science can't give an answer to the question, "Why should I be good?"',[60] while the atheistic journalist Natasha Walter admitted on BBC Television's *Soul of Britain,* 'I don't think any scientist would say that it was for science to say what is ethically right to do.'[61]

Science is not able to answer life's deepest questions

Steve Jones, an avowed materialist, freely admits this in his book *The Language of the Genes:* 'Science cannot answer the questions that philosophers — or children — ask: why are we here, what is the point of being alive, how ought we to behave? Genetics has almost nothing to say about what makes us more than machines driven by biology, about what makes us human. These questions may be interesting, but scientists are no more qualified to comment on them than is anyone else.'[62] Sir John Eccles, a Nobel Prize-winning pioneer in brain research, pinpointed some of these issues: 'Science cannot explain the existence of each of us as a unique self, nor can it answer such fundamental questions as "Who am I? How did I come to be at a certain place and time? What happens after death?" These are all mysteries beyond science.'[63] The eminent psychiatrist Paul Tournier came to the same conclusion: 'Everybody today is searching for an answer to those problems to which science pays no attention, the problem of their destiny, the mystery of evil, the question of death.'[64]

These are among the most fundamental questions we could ever ask — and in response, science can only shrug its shoulders and pass them elsewhere. Even the world-renowned Austrian philosopher and mathematician Ludwig Wittgenstein admitted, 'We feel that even when all possible scientific questions have been answered, the problems of life remain completely untouched.'[65] Quantum theory expert Erwin Schrödinger said much the same thing: 'I am very astonished that the scientific picture of the world around me is very deficient. It gives a lot of factual information, puts all our experience in a magnificently consistent order, but is ghastly silent about all and sundry that is really near to our heart ... it knows nothing about beautiful and ugly, good or bad, God and eternity. Science sometimes pretends to answer questions in these domains, but the answers are very often so silly that we are not inclined to take them seriously.'[66]

The ultimate issue

Several years ago, *Encyclopaedia Britannica* published a set of fifty-four volumes pulling together the writings of many eminent thinkers on the most important ideas that men have studied and investigated over the centuries. The topics chosen included law, science, philosophy and history, but the longest essay of all was on the subject of God. Addressing the question as to why this should be the case, co-editor Mortimer Adler, the American philosopher and author, wrote, 'More consequences for thought and action follow from the affirmation or denial of God than from answering any other question.'[67] Adler was obviously right, yet science is unable to decide the issue, or even to address the question.

We need not deal with *scientism* here. As we saw in the last chapter, it is not even open to the suggestion that God might exist — it 'cannot allow a Divine foot in the door' — but to approach the subject having already decided the answer to the question hardly qualifies as being honest, let alone reasonable. Our concern is with true science, which depends on the use of repeatable observations or experiments with consistent results *not manipulated in any way by the world-view of those making or conducting them.* Science is uncovering an amazing amount of fascinating information about the wonder and vastness of God's creation and the ways in which natural laws function, yet there are three obvious reasons why molecular biologist Andrew Miller is right to say, 'It is certainly not a scientific matter to decide whether or not there is a God.'[68]

The God revealed in the Bible has no physical or material dimensions or characteristics

In other words, he has none of the properties belonging to matter. In the Bible's own words, 'God is spirit';[69] that is to say, he has no 'parts'. He is simple, as opposed to complex; indivisible as well as invisible. This means that while science can examine creation it cannot examine the Creator. Sir Gabriel Horn, Head of Zoology at Cambridge University, draws an obvious inference: 'Scientists seek to understand the universe … through observation and experiment. Science is an empirical discipline. So far as I am aware, no empirical tests have been devised that provide compelling evidence to refute the existence of God.'[70]

God transcends the realm in which science operates

A second and related reason why science is unable to disprove God's existence is that, although he permeates every nook and cranny of the universe, he is uniquely transcendent — over, above and beyond time, space and all finite reality. I am writing this as NASA's Mars Exploration Rovers — Opportunity and Spirit — are sending fascinating data back to earth after epic journeys of 250 million miles to the 'red planet'. Yet God cannot be 'reached' in this way, however sophisticated the technology. He is distinct and separate from the entire universe and everything in it, and can no more be confined to space than he can be measured by time. He is essentially 'other' than creation, so outside of all reality that is open to scientific investigation. The Bible records God as saying:

> For my thoughts are not your thoughts,
>   neither are your ways my ways…
> As the heavens are higher than the earth,
>   so are my ways higher than your ways
>   and my thoughts than your thoughts. [71]

It is impossible for any scientist operating entirely within the natural world to make any discovery in the realm of the supernatural. In Michael Poole's words, 'You cannot measure the beauty of a sunset with a multimeter. Neither is it any use asking science whether there is a God. Science is the study of the physical world. *Questions about God are outside its terms of reference.'*[72]

It is impossible to prove a universal negative

For someone to prove the non-existence of God would mean that person being in possession of every single fact in all of reality. If even one fact was not known, God's existence could not be ruled out, as it might be the fact in question. God is clearly a possible fact and to say that science is able to rule him out of existence flies in the face of common sense. Peter Atkins told the atheist (and strangely named!) *Free Inquiry Magazine*, 'Science is progressively advancing toward complete knowledge, leaving religions bobbing in its wake,'[73] but to suggest that 'complete knowledge' is attainable is naïve, while the rest of the sentence is nonsense.

Nothing that has been written in this chapter is to be taken as a criticism of science. As we saw in the opening paragraphs, science is a success story, and growing more successful every day. It is an exciting, elevating exercise in which we can take great pleasure and from which we can derive great benefit. We should thank God for scientists — even those who deny his existence — but we do not honour science by ignoring its intrinsic limitations and pretending that it can explain everything.

4.
Evolution: proof or prejudice?

In the supposed war between science and Christianity over the last 400 years the names of two men, an Italian and an Englishman, have often been used as heavy artillery by those on the side of science. The first name is now reduced to little more than a distant echo, and for our present purposes the issue in which he was involved can be dealt with very briefly; the second is still being heard loud and clear whenever science and religion are said to come into conflict.

The Italian

Galileo Galilei (now simply known as Galileo) was born in Pisa in 1564. He earned a reputation as a philosopher and physicist, but his contribution to science and religion was as an astronomer — some have even suggested that he was 'the father of astronomy'. Ancient Greek philosophers such as Aristotle and Plato taught that Earth sat fixed at the centre of the entire universe, with all the other heavenly bodies circling around it. This idea was endorsed by the influential second-century Egyptian astronomer and geographer Claudius Ptolemy and was not seriously questioned for another 1,400 years, when the

Polish astronomer and mathematician Nicolaus Copernicus shocked the world by insisting that, within an even vaster universe, the *sun* was at the centre of a massive planetary system of which Earth was merely a part.

Enter Galileo. Using a state-of-the-art telescope he had built, Galileo decided that Copernicus was right, and in his *Dialogue of the Two Great Systems of the Universe*, published in 1616, declared that Earth rotates on its own axis and revolves around the sun. This got him into serious trouble with the (Roman Catholic) Church, which believed it had a monopoly on all truth and accused him of contradicting what the Bible taught. Although Galileo protested that the Bible was intended 'to teach us how one goes to heaven, not how heaven goes' and that 'Two truths cannot contradict each other,' the church turned up the heat. One Dominican Father preached that 'Geometry is of the devil' and that 'Mathematics should be banished as the author of all heresies' — and was promptly promoted! Other religious leaders said that Galileo's ideas upset 'the whole basis of theology', including God's plan of salvation. The case became entangled with a variety of unsavoury religious politics and in 1633 Galileo was hauled before the notorious Inquisition, which had been set up to deal with heretics. Publication of all his works was banned and only his poor health caused his death sentence to be commuted to imprisonment for life.

These are the bare bones of a story some people still use as a trigger for the idea that science has disposed of God: that the church refused to accept scientific progress, but Galileo was right; that science beat Christianity hands down and has been a superior source of truth ever since. However, to draw this conclusion is to play fast and loose with the facts. Firstly, Galileo's argument was not so much with the church as with seventeenth-century science as a whole. In other words, the debate was not between Galileo and religion, but between scientists who refused to move with the times and who believed that the sun (and all the other heavenly bodies) moved around the Earth, on the one hand, and those who believed that within a vaster universe Earth moved around the sun, on the other. Secondly, even after he had come to his scientific conclusions, Galileo had no dispute with the Bible or the existence of God. Thirdly, to decide that God is non-existent because seventeenth-century theologians wrongly claimed that the Bible endorsed a faulty scientific model dreamed up by ancient Greek philosophers is neither good science nor good sense.

The Englishman

In 2002, BBC Television ran a survey to find 'the greatest Briton of them all'. Nominees included William Shakespeare, Sir Winston Churchill, Sir Isaac Newton, Oliver Cromwell and Queen Elizabeth I, but television journalist Andrew Marr had no doubts as to how the voting should go: 'In all its history Britain has only one world-changer. His name is Charles Darwin.'[1] Before the poll was held, Richard Dawkins wrote that Darwin ranked alongside Newton and Shakespeare as 'Britain's greatest gift to the world' and that '… his guiding genius hovers over all of modern history.'[2]

Their hero had a stuttering start to his adult life. After failing to make the grade as a medical student, and doing poorly when he switched to classics and mathematics, he eventually graduated from Cambridge with a B.A. in theology. His father had hoped that Charles would enter the Church of England ministry, but the young man had no stomach for this and was more or less at a loose end when in 1831, in spite of having had no relevant training, he was offered a place as a naturalist on the survey ship HMS *Beagle*, about to set sail on a five-year expedition.

Prior to joining *Beagle*, Darwin seems to have gone along with the almost universally accepted belief that, as Creator of the entire universe, God had brought into being all the world's different living species, with independent characteristics suited to their environment. But as the journey went on, Darwin increasingly questioned the fixity of species and eventually became convinced that entirely new species could arise by natural descent from pre-existing ones. For over twenty-five years after *Beagle* returned to England he worked on the manuscript of what would have been a massive volume on the subject. This never saw the light of day, but in 1859, concerned by news that the British naturalist and biologist Alfred Wallace was about to go into print along similar lines, he rushed out a condensed version of his notes under the title *The Origin of Species by Means of Natural Selection or the Preservation of Favoured Species,* now usually referred to as *The Origin of Species* or simply *Origin.* Early indications gave no inkling that it was to be anything other than a collection of interesting ideas by an amateur naturalist. The *Daily News* thought that Darwin was merely repeating what had been said by the Scottish publisher and natural philosopher Robert Chambers in a book published fifteen years earlier and already in its eleventh edition. The editor of the prestigious *Quarterly Review* suggested that if Darwin wanted to become famous he should abandon *Origin* and write a book on pigeons! Even his publisher, John Murray, an amateur geologist, had serious doubts about whether to go ahead with it because he considered Darwin's main theory 'as absurd as though one should contemplate a fruitful union between a poker and a rabbit'.[3]

One of the book's most highly qualified critics was Adam Sedgwick, Woodwardian Professor of Geology at Trinity College, Cambridge, and one of the founders of geology as a science in England. In a letter to Darwin he wrote, 'I have read your book with more pain than pleasure. Parts of it I admired greatly, parts I laughed at till my sides were almost sore; other parts I read with absolute sorrow because I think them utterly false and grievously mischievous.'[4]

A bombshell

The doubters were soon sidelined and within twenty years the book's major thesis, although since described as nothing more than 'a highly speculative hypothesis',[5] had become all the rage, and in its overview of the twentieth century *TIME* Magazine said, 'Darwinism remains one of the most successful scientific theories ever promulgated.'[6] No other theory about life on earth has done more to affect the way people think about themselves and their relationship to other people and to the world around them. The British biologist Sir Julian Huxley called it 'the most powerful and most comprehensive idea that has ever arisen on earth'.[7] In the definitive modern biography of Darwin, James Moore writes, 'More than any modern thinker — even Freud or Marx — [Darwin]… has transformed the way we see ourselves on this planet.'[8] Darwinism in one form or another has become a total philosophy which claims to explain the origin and development of everything in the world and is so pervasive that physicist H. S. Lipton calls *Origin* 'perhaps the most influential book that has ever been published'.[9]

Ironically, the word most often used in employing Darwin's theory as a weapon against God does not even appear in the first edition of *Origin*. That word is 'evolution'. Biology classifies living things according to their similarities. The largest grouping is the 'domain' (e.g. eucarya); domains are divided into 'kingdoms' (e.g. animals); kingdoms into 'phyla' (e.g. chordates); phyla into 'classes' (e.g. mammals); classes into orders (e.g. primates), and so on down through families, genera and finally species, though the precise divisions are not universally agreed. On the face of it, there is nothing about the idea of evolution that should have caused even a tremor in religious, philosophical or scientific circles. It was already widely accepted that great variations occurred *within* existing species and families by perfectly natural processes. Although Darwin called this model (micro-evolution) his 'special theory', it added little or nothing to what was already known and accepted. What turned his book into a bombshell was what is now called his 'general theory' — *macro-evolution.*

Put very simply, macro-evolution says that all the world's life-forms are linked seamlessly together in a natural process of evolution, one species arising from another by spontaneous, random, natural means, without any external power or direction, in an unbroken chain going right back to a single spark of life that appeared on our planet at some point in prehistory. The British writer and researcher Ian Taylor makes this clear: 'The idea that life on earth originated from a single-celled organism and then progressed onwards and upwards in ever-increasing complexity to culminate in man himself is what the theory of evolution is all about.'[10] In *Origin,* man was not in fact included in the model, but in *The Descent of Man,* published in 1871, Darwin bit the bullet and wrote, 'The main conclusion arrived at ... is that *man is descended from some less highly organized form.*'[11] To underline his point he added that humankind has survived '*not according to some ordered plan* but as a result of chance operating among countless creatures by nature's unlimited tendency towards variation'.[12]

The entire package is now taken for granted by countless millions of people and a great deal of modern academic thought is governed by the assumption that all living phenomena have to be seen in evolutionary terms. In 1996 the celebrated geneticist H. J. Muller circulated a manifesto signed by 177 American biologists asserting that organic evolution of all living things, man included, from primitive life-forms, and even from non-living materials, is a fact of science as well established as the fact that the earth is round.[13] The biologist Ernst Mayr, Professor Emeritus at Harvard University, writes, 'Since Darwin, every knowing person agrees man descended from the apes. Today, there is no such thing as the theory of evolution. It is the fact of evolution.'[14] Richard Dawkins endorses this verdict with a typically truculent flourish: 'It is absolutely safe to say that if you meet somebody who does not believe in evolution, that person is ignorant, stupid or insane (or wicked, but I'd rather not consider that).'[15]

Today, Darwin's idea dominates the entire philosophical, scientific and cultural landscape, yet one of its greatest and most radical effects is religious. In *Origin*, Darwin made a few token allusions to God, but Adam Sedgwick saw past these and anticipated where the book was leading: 'From first to last it is a dish of rank materialism cleverly cooked and served up ... and why is this done? For no other solid reason, I am sure, except to make us independent of a Creator.'[16] Addressing a conference held in 1959 to mark the centenary of the first publication of *Origin*, Sir Julian Huxley said, 'Darwin's real achievement was to remove the whole idea of God as the Creator of organisms from the sphere of rational discussion.'[17] In recent times, the same point has often been made by those who have studied Darwin's work. The Australian molecular biologist and physician Michael Denton wrote, 'The decline in religious belief can probably be attributed more to the propagation and advocacy by the intellectual and scientific community of the Darwinian version of evolution than to any other single factor.'[18] Richard Dawkins has since said, 'Although atheism might have been logically tenable before Darwin, Darwin made it possible to be an intellectually fulfilled atheist,'[19] while on the last day of 1999, *TIME* Magazine made this dramatic assessment: 'Charles Darwin didn't want to murder God. But he did.' [20]

From zoo to you?

These impressive-sounding claims need to be faced, as so much hinges on their truth or falsehood. As we have seen, the Darwinian model of evolution, taking in all living organisms, begins with the first spark of life, but we shall try to unpack it 'from the outside in', beginning with human beings. How did *we* become what we are? The idea that our immediate ancestors were apelike mammals is now so commonly held that it is generally taken for granted. In 1994, the Arts and Entertainment Network aired a television programme in the United States with the title *Ape Man: The Story of Human Evolution*. The programme was anchored by the well-known broadcaster Walter Cronkite, who put the popular notion in this down-to earth way: 'If you go back far enough, we and the chimps have a common ancestor. My father's father's father's father's father, going back maybe half a million generations — about five million years — was an ape.'[21] We can safely assume that millions of viewers accepted Cronkite's words with the same confidence as they did his dramatic announcement thirty-one years earlier that President John F. Kennedy had been assassinated in Dallas — but on this occasion he was not able to produce a shred of evidence to confirm the claim.

Nobody seriously denies that apes and humans share some physical characteristics, and have similar DNA, but that is a long way from proving a direct link between the two species. There is a huge gap between similarities and direct relationship. Haemoglobin, the molecule that carries oxygen in red blood cells, is to be found not only in humans but also in earthworms, starfish, molluscs, in some insects and plants, and even in certain bacteria. Does this mean that they, too, are our immediate ancestors? Some of the data in this field are more confusing than confirming. When scientists examined the haemoglobin of crocodiles, vipers and chickens, they found that the crocodiles were more closely linked to the chickens than to their fellow reptiles,[22] while in another test an identical protein was found on the cell wall of both camels and nurse sharks.[23]

The model that sees *Homo sapiens* as evolution's crowning glory is often backed up by diagrams and drawings showing how we emerged from a succession of stooped, hairy creatures. These artists' impressions are often brilliantly done and superficially persuasive, but they are largely the result of guesswork based on evolutionary assumptions, and time and again their message has been discredited by scientific discoveries. This has been especially true in the field of palaeontology, the study of fossils, which has blown huge holes in the 'monkey to man' scenario. Here are just five of many well-known examples that can be cited:

1. In 1857, quarrymen found a partial skeleton in a cave near Düsseldorf in Germany. The bones seemed to be human, but when similar remains were found in Europe, Africa and Asia they were given the common name Neanderthal and said to be pre-human. Artists and others got to work and produced semi-erect, barrel-chested models with short legs, massive eyebrow ridges and strong lower jaws. The complete package was then presented as evidence of a link between humans and some primitive intermediate creature.

However, the idea was dealt a fatal blow when a Ne-anderthal skeleton, buried in a relatively modern suit of armour, was found in a tomb in Poland in 1908.[24] Today, DNA evidence indicates that Neanderthal was 'a card-carrying member of the human family'[25] after all, and a recent book suggests, 'If a Neanderthal were dressed in jeans and a T-shirt, and went to a ball game, you and I would probably not notice him or her.'[26] The idea that Neanderthal is a 'missing link' has since been quietly dropped from textbooks.

2. In 1912, Charles Dawson, an amateur fossil hunter, took a collection of bones, teeth and primitive instru-ments to a friend at the British Museum, claiming to have found them in a gravel pit near Piltdown, in Sussex. Sci-entists declared the remains to be 500,000 years old and the so-called Piltdown Man was touted as 'the sensational missing link',[27] the three scientists responsible for promot-ing him receiving knighthoods for their work. But in 1953 their hero was proved to be a hoax, consisting of a human skull, the lower jaw of an orang-utan and the teeth of a chimpanzee.

3. In 1922, a single tooth unearthed in Nebraska was enthusiastically claimed to be from an early type of Pithecanthropoid (apelike man) who lived between 1.7 and 5.5 million years ago. The *Illustrated London News* published a double-page feature trumpeting Nebraska Man as a vital link in the 'monkey to man' chain, but six years later it was discovered that the tooth had come from a peccary, a pig-like wild animal. The Nebraska Man claim now shares the peccary's state of extinction, but together they are a good illustration of the comment made by Professor Bolton Davidheiser of Johns Hopkins University: 'The non-scientific public has great faith in what a palaeontologist can do with a single bone.'[28]

4. In 1959, the well-known palaeontologist Louis Leakey and his wife Mary exhumed an interesting skull in East Africa. Dubbed 'Nutcracker Man' because of its huge jaw, it was first dated at 1.75 million years, making it by far the oldest hominoid fossil ever found, but this claim was torpedoed when further bones found *lower down* were dated at only just over 10,000 years. Leakey eventually withdrew his extravagant claim and conceded that his find was one of many *Australopithecus africanus,* now believed to be extinct African apes.

5. In 1974 the American anthropologist Donald Johanson found a tiny skeleton in the Great Rift Valley, Ethiopia. Nicknamed 'Lucy', it was dated at three million years and became a sensation when announced at the Nobel Symposium on Early Man in 1978. Lucy was hailed as the first ape to walk upright and an undoubted link between apes and humans, but in a question-and-answer session at the University of Missouri in 1996, Johanson admitted that the knee joint cited as proof that Lucy walked upright had been found more than two miles away and 200 feet lower in the strata! Richard Leakey, Director of Kenya's National Museum, decided that '… the evidence for the alleged transformation from

ape to man is extremely unconvincing,' and that '… it is overwhelmingly likely that Lucy was no more than a variety of pygmy chimpanzee.'[29] Johanson eventually withdrew his original claim and concluded that Lucy was not related to humans after all.[30]

These are just some of the high-profile cases put forward as evidence that *Homo sapiens* evolved from apelike ancestors, yet, along with hundreds of other attempts, they have failed to make the case. Dr D. V. Ager, President of the British Geological Association, makes this important point: 'It must be significant that nearly all the evolutionary stories I learned as a student have now been debunked… The point emerges that, if we examine the fossil record in detail, whether at the level of order or of species, we find — over and over again — not gradual evolution, but the sudden explosion of one group at the expense of another.'[31]

Human evolution from apelike ancestors is so loudly and persistently taught that it has become a given in society at large. Virtually every radio and television programme dealing with the natural sciences assumes it to be true, and anyone raising a voice against it is likely to be treated as an eccentric, to say the least. Yet any protester has good company among authorities in the field. The distinguished palaeoanthropologist David Pilbeam, Professor of Anthropology at Harvard University, candidly admits, 'Perhaps generations of students of human evolution, including myself, have been flailing about in the dark … our database is too sparse, too slippery, for it to be able to mould our theories. Rather, the theories are more statements about us and [our] ideology than about the past.'[32] Elsewhere, he is even more specific: 'There is no clear-cut and inexorable pathway from ape to man.'[33] Having spent twenty-five years researching the fossil record, the American scholar Marvin Lubenow opened his book *Bones of Contention* with the words: 'The human fossil record is strongly supportive of the concept of Special Creation. On the other hand, the fossil record is so contrary to human evolution as to *effectively falsify the idea that humans evolved.*'[34] Later, he added, 'Human evolution allegedly took place in the past over vast periods of time. Evolutionists readily admit that evolutionary processes work so slowly that they are not observable over the lifetime of one individual or even over the successive lifetimes of hundreds of generations. In other words, *there are no direct observations or experiments that can confirm the process of human evolution.*'[35]

In all of this, we need to recognize that the issue is not the fossils themselves, but their interpretation. The hard-core evolutionist puts his theory before the facts and goes to the fossil record governed by his theory and looking to have it confirmed by what he finds. In 1991, a spokesman for the American Association for the Advancement of Science went so far as to say that 100 million fossils, identified and dated, 'constitute 100 million facts that prove evolution beyond any doubt whatsoever'.[36] The problem with this statement is that the fossil record has been assessed *on the assumption that macro-evolution is an established fact.* But this is a clear example of circular reasoning, leading one professor of anthropology to say, 'The problem with a lot of anthropologists is that they want so much to find a hominid that any scrap of bone becomes a hominid bone.'[37] David Pilbeam confesses, 'I know that, at least in palaeoanthropology, data are still so sparse that theory heavily influences interpretations. Theories have, in the past, clearly reflected our current ideologies instead of the actual data.'[38] If we keep to the facts, palaeontology tells us that whenever we discover human fossils — and thousands have been found — they are already fully human, with no signs of transition from a more primitive creature. After many years of research in this particular field, the distinguished anatomist Lord Zuckerman, Chief Scientific Adviser to the British government, concluded that '… if man evolved from an apelike creature, he did so without leaving a trace of that evolution in the fossil record.'[39] There are no apes in human history.

Quite apart from what the fossil evidence tells us, those who insist that we *did* descend from apelike ancestors run headlong into a barrage of questions. If we are only the products of blind, mindless chance, how can we claim to have greater dignity than snakes or seaweed, vegetation or viruses? Why are we inescapably self-conscious? Why should we imagine that our lives have any meaning or purpose? Why do we long for significance? What motivates our goals and aspirations? How can we claim greater rights than buffalo or bacteria? Why do we insist on living within some kind of moral framework, even if we occasionally tweak it to our personal advantage? If we are nothing more than shrink-wrapped bags of biological elements governed by the laws of physics, how do we account for the existence and authority of conscience? Why do we know that there is a radical difference between good and evil? How did we acquire a sense of humour, or an interest in aesthetics? Why do we seem to have an eradicable spiritual dimension? Why do we think (more often than we care to admit) about death? Is there an evolutionary answer to these questions — some biological or chemical accident that can explain their existence?

In an earlier chapter we noted that the humanist scholar Edmund Leach went so far as to claim, 'There is no sharp break between what is human and what is mechanical,' but this was a clear case of bending the facts to fit the philosophy. The break between man and all other material reality is vast. We have no evolutionary ancestors.

Fatal flaws

The general theory of evolution says that we are the latest product of a 'Great Chain of Being', with non-living matter, then protozoans (microscopic, single-cell organisms), metazoan invertebrates (multi-celled organisms without a backbone or spinal column), vertebrate fishes, amphibians, reptiles, birds, furry quadrupeds and apes forming our 'family tree'. There is no space here to look at each of these in turn, but there are at least five factors that reveal huge flaws in this widely accepted scenario.

1. The missing links

The first is the fact that, just as in the case of the 'monkey-to-man' idea, *the 'missing links' are still missing*! Concerned about the absence of intermediate links between species, Darwin admitted that this was 'the most obvious and serious objection that could be urged against [his] theory', but decided that this could be explained by 'the extreme imperfection of the geological record'.[40] We are now in a very different position, with a vastly greater number of fossils at our disposal, yet David Raup, Curator of Geology at Chicago's Field Museum of Natural History, states, 'The situation hasn't changed much. The record of evolution is still surprisingly jerky and, ironically, *we now have even fewer examples of evolutionary transition than we had in Darwin's time... Darwin's problem has not been alleviated.*'[41] Stephen J. Gould, Professor of Geology and Palaeontology at Harvard University, has no hesitation in saying that the extreme rarity of transitional forms in the fossil record 'persists as the trade secret of palaeontology'.[42] Niles Eldredge, Moderator of the American Museum of Natural History, confirms the conspiracy: 'We palaeontologists have said that the history of life supports ... [the story of gradual adaptive change] ... *all the while knowing that it does not.*'[43] Since the evidence from palaeontology is the only one that claims to present proof of the history of evolution, rather than its results and mechanisms, Raup's admission is particularly important, as Darwin had hoped that the discovery of further fossils would reveal the missing links needed to confirm his theory. Although we now have a staggering number of fossils to examine, Darwin's own conclusion — 'Not one change of species into another is on record ... we cannot prove that a single species has been changed'[44]— remains essentially correct, though in the modern context we should probably replace his word 'species' by a somewhat broader grouping.

2. 'Typing errors'

The second flaw concerns the mechanism said to drive evo-lution. Darwin leaned heavily on what he called 'natural selection', which originally said that organisms prey on each other in order to survive and at the same time develop new characteristics in order to cope with their environment. When these characteristics become permanent features, a new species emerges in what Darwin called 'progress towards perfection'. This leads to the concept of 'the survival of the fittest', a phrase Darwin adapted from the British philosopher Herbert Spencer's *Principles of Biology*, published in 1865 and included from the sixth edition of *Origin* onwards.

But by the 1930s it had become obvious to biologists that natural selection alone could never produce organic macro-evolution. It might provide a good model for changes *within* species and families, but not for the creation of new ones. Macro-evolution needed a new ingredient; biologists proposed the 'synthetic theory', so called because it merged classical Darwinism and modern genetic ideas. The theory centred on the genes and proposed that if over an immense amount of time these underwent radical, inheritable changes — mutations — nature could use those most suitable for future development, leading eventually to the creation of new orders of animals. *No such transformations have ever been observed*. Instead, they are inferred on the basis of the circular argument that this is how new orders arise according to evolutionary theory.

Nevertheless, this new model, under the general name of neo-Darwinianism, has so completely taken over that Sylvia Baker, a respected writer in the field, goes so far as to say that 'The modern theory of evolution … stands or falls on this question of mutation.'[45]

If this is the case, the theory is very unsteady on its feet! In the first place, natural mutations occur *extremely rarely*, something like once in every ten million duplications of a DNA molecule.[46] Even a staunch evolutionist like Sir Julian Huxley says that the odds against favourable mutations occurring in one strain through pure chance are so long that it would take three large-format volumes of about 500 pages to print them out. No wonder he adds, 'No one would bet on anything so improbable happening.'[47]

Secondly, 999 out of every 1,000 mutations are *harmful*, weakening or destroying the organism concerned, rather than creating the advantageous changes needed for evolution. In fact, organisms from bacteria to humans have DNA mismatch repair systems consisting of more than a dozen separate proteins which scan the genome (the entire complement of genetic material in an individual set of chromosomes) for 'mistakes' (mutations) or damage induced by environmental factors, and either repair them or target the cell to be removed. Such mechanisms have no means of being selective and will act with equal efficiency to nullify both harmful and the much rarer 'useful' mutations. It seems curious that a process so critical to evolution should generate largely deleterious changes and then be subject to a complex biological preventative mechanism.

Noting that a mutation is a random change in a molecular message (DNA), the Canadian medical professor Magnus Verbrugge likens it to a typing error and adds, 'Typing errors rarely improve the quality of a written message; if too many occur, they may even destroy the message contained in it.'[48]

Phillip Johnson uses another illustration to make the same point: 'To suppose that such a random event could reconstruct even a single complex organ like a liver or kidney is about as reasonable as to suppose that an improved watch can be designed by throwing an old one against a wall.'[49]

Thirdly, *the time needed* for mutations to trigger a new species is simply not available. The French biologist Rémy Chauvin, Professor in the Laboratory of Animal Sociology at

René Descartes University, Paris, says, 'Since those forms of animal life which mutate very rapidly have remained the same during tens of millions of generations, *mutations could not be considered the motor of evolution.*' Significantly, he goes on, 'This is a matter of good sense, but given the strength of prejudice within science as everywhere else, good sense loses its case in court.'[50]

The biochemist Sir Ernest Chain, co-holder of the 1945 Nobel Prize for developing penicillin, was equally dismissive: 'To postulate that the development and survival of the fittest is entirely a consequence of chance mutations seems to me a hypothesis based on no evidence and irreconcilable with the facts. These classical evolutionary theories are a gross over-simplification of an immensely complex and intricate mass of facts, and it amazes me that they are swallowed so uncritically and readily, and for such a long time, by so many scientists, without a murmur of protest.'[51]

3. Incomplete means useless

A third flaw in the macro-evolution model is that any new, functional organ has to be a complete, operating entity before it can be of any benefit to the organism concerned. This clashes head-on with evolution's claim that mutation takes place in tiny increments over a vast amount of time. The human eye provides a good illustration. It comes with automatic aiming, focusing and aperture adjustment and its tiny retina has 130 million receptor cells, 124 million of which are rod-shaped and differentiate between light and darkness, and six million of which are cone-shaped and can identify up to eight million variations of colour. Is it possible that all of these features came into being by means of the genetic equivalent of typing errors over millions of years? Those who insist that this is the case (and Darwin did, in spite of admitting that for natural selection to form the eye was 'absurd in the highest possible degree')[52] have surely missed the point that a partial eye is useless. Five per cent of an eye would not give five per cent vision — it would give none. What is more, even if all the physical components of an eye were in place, they would achieve nothing unless they were precisely 'wired' to an amazing complex of nerve cells in the brain. Small wonder that someone has suggested, 'Examination of the eye is a cure for atheism.'[53]

4. Irreducible complexity

A fourth flaw is linked to the third and has to do with irreducible complexity. Darwin once wrote, 'If it could be demonstrated that any complex organ existed which could not possibly have been formed by numerous, successive, slight modifications, *my theory would absolutely break down. But I can find no such case.*'[54] He said this knowing nothing of the marvels revealed by modern microbiology. To Darwin and his contemporaries the biological cell was nothing more than a mysterious 'blob' of protoplasm, which they had no instruments to examine in detail. Microbiology has now opened this 'black box' of ignorance and revealed a world of staggering complexity; we know, for example that even relatively simple bacteria cells can synthesize up to 6,000 compounds at a rate of a million reactions per second.[55]

In his runaway best-seller *Darwin's Black Box*, first published in 1996, Michael Behe, Professor of Biological Sciences at Lehigh University, Pennsylvania, goes significantly further and identifies numerous examples of irreducible complexity that could not possibly have evolved. As Behe explains, something is irreducibly complex 'if it's composed of several parts and each part is absolutely necessary for the structure to function'.[56] As a brilliant example he cites blood-clotting, which involves a very complex, intricately woven system consisting of a score of independent protein parts. He shows that in the case of an invasive event (a cut) a protein which is found only on the outside of cells not in contact with the blood is brought into the bloodstream locally and triggers off an ordered cascade of events, involving twenty-eight separate proteins and enzymes, which results in localized clotting and the sealing of the wound.

The all-important point about the whole process, which Behe describes in great detail, is that the cascade is formed in a specific way with a defined number of known interacting molecules. In other words, it is an irreducibly complex system, precisely the kind of thing Darwin admitted would destroy his whole evolutionary system. If natural selection is to produce a fully functioning, irreducibly complex system, it has to do it all at once. Yet Behe says that even a tiny part of such a system coming together by genetic mutation 'would not be expected to happen even if the universe's ten-billion year life were compressed into a single second and relived every second for ten billion years'.[57]

5. The Cambrian conundrum

A fifth flaw is that evolutionism has no answer to the so-called Cambrian Explosion. Over the last 150 years or so, most scientists have revised the supposed age of our planet from a few thousand years to about 4,600 million years. Using this time-scale, it has been found that an absence of evidence for life-forms prior to 600 million years ago suddenly gives way to a huge number of fossils representing nearly every group of organisms alive today and *without any sign of evolutionary ancestors*. To make matters worse for evolutionists, fossils of highly complex life-forms far outnumber those of the simplest ones and include those representing every one of the major invertebrates. Using their own time-frame, evolutionists estimate that such complex creatures would have required at least 1.5 billion years to evolve, yet there is no pre-Cambrian evidence in support of any such evolution having taken place. As even Richard Dawkins admits, 'It is as though they were just planted there, without any evolutionary history.'[58] Phillip Johnson may not be wide of the mark when he describes the Cambrian explosion as 'the greatest single problem which the fossil record poses for Darwinianism'.[59]

These are among the most damaging blows to the macro-evolution hypothesis. The American mathematician and physicist Wolfgang Smith summed up their significance: 'We are told dogmatically that evolution is an established fact; but we are never told who established it, and by what means. We are told, often enough, that the doctrine is founded upon evidence ... but we are left entirely in the dark on the crucial question wherein, precisely, this evidence consists.'[60] Later he adds, 'If by evolution we mean macro-evolution ... it can be said with the utmost rigour that the doctrine is totally bereft of scientific sanction ... there exists today not a shred of *bona fide* scientific evidence in support of the thesis that macro-evolution transformations have ever occurred.'[61]

Dr Marcel P. Schutzenberger, Professor of the Faculty of Sciences at the University of Paris, was equally dismissive. In *Mathematical Challenges to the neo-Darwinian Theory of Evolution*, he concluded that the probability of evolution based on mutation and natural selection was 'not conceivable' because there is 'no chance ... to see this mechanism appear spontaneously and, if it did, even less for it to remain... We believe there is a considerable gap in the neo-Darwinian Theory of evolution, and we believe this gap to be of such a nature that it cannot be bridged with the current conception of biology.'[62]

In 1980, some 150 of the world's leading evolutionary theorists met at the University of Chicago for a conference 'to consider the mechanisms that underlie the origin of species'. A subsequent report stated, 'The central question of the Chicago conference was whether the mechanisms underlying micro-evolution can be extrapolated to explain the phenomena of macro-evolution ... the answer can be given as a clear, "No".'[63]

One other point needs to be made, which is that macro-evolution claims to explain the present characteristics of living things, *whatever those characteristics may be*, but it is incapable

of giving us a fundamental explanation of how these characteristics came about. The Cambridge scholar R. E. D. Clark makes
the point like this: 'Evolutionary explanations are almost entirely
of the after-the-event kind. The camel has a hump and this like
everything else is due to natural selection which we are told
offers "a scientific rational mechanistic explanation". Maybe,
but if the camel had no hump, the explanation would be the
same. The cat has a tail and natural selection tells us why. But if
puss had no tail, natural selection would explain that too. If an
animal has a feature which seems to confer no obvious advantage, we are told that it must have an advantage or it would not
be there. If difficulties are raised we are told that the advantage
lies in some other factor with which the first is genetically linked
and *oleiogenes* are invented for the purpose... If a feature
which would be useful to an animal is *not* there, then of course
natural selection explains this too. And so on, whatever the facts
to be explained... Nevertheless [this] does not get us very far.
After all, natural selection also determines which cars remain on
the roads after a lapse of time and which disappear, but this
does not tell us how the models are manufactured.'[64]

The first spark

As we track backwards through the evolutionary model we
inevitably arrive at the point at which we need to find an
explanation for the origin of life itself. To become a starting-
point for an ongoing evolutionary process, such a life-form
would need to store genetic information, process energy and
replicate — three things that non-living systems are incapable of
doing. The obvious problem is therefore how to get life started;
those who rule God out of the equation have turned to the only
alternative — spontaneous generation.

As Darwin wrestled with the problem he fantasized about
'some warm little pond, with all sorts of ammonia and phosphoric
salts, light, heat, electricity, etc. present', in which 'a protein

compound was chemically formed ready to undergo still more complex changes'.[65] Since then, numerous experiments have been carried out to see if life could have been spontaneously generated in some kind of primordial 'soup', but at best these have been able to produce nothing more than a few basic amino-acids, the building blocks of proteins. Yet even an unlimited supply of proteins would not come close to producing a living cell.

In *The Intelligent Universe*, Sir Fred Hoyle makes the point like this: 'If there were a basic principle of matter which somehow drove organic systems toward life, its existence should easily be demonstrable in the laboratory. One could, for instance, take a swimming bath to represent the primordial soup. Fill it with any chemicals of a non-biological nature you please. Pump any gases over it, or through it, you please, and shine any kind of radiation on it that takes your fancy. Let the experiment proceed for a year and see how many of those 2,000 enzymes [the 'worker' proteins found in living cells] have appeared in the bath. I will give the answer, and so save the time and trouble and expense of actually doing the experiment. You would find nothing at all except perhaps for a tarry sludge composed of amino-acids and other simple organic chemicals. How can I be so confident of this statement? Well, if it were otherwise, the experiment would long since have been done and would be well-known and famous throughout the world. The cost of it would be trivial compared to the cost of landing a man on the Moon ... in short, there is not a shred of objective evidence to support the hypothesis that life began in an organic soup here on the Earth.'[66]

This is hardly surprising when one considers the massive difference between life and non-life and the creative capacity that the most primitive of cells would have needed to survive and reproduce. Michael Denton hits the nail on the head when he says, 'We now know not only of the existence of a break between the living and the non-living world, but also that it represents the most dramatic and fundamental of all the discontinuities of nature. Between a living cell and the most highly ordered non-biological system, such as a crystal or a snowflake, there is a chasm as vast and absolute as it is possible to conceive.'[67] He then adds, 'Although the tiniest bacterial cells are incredibly small, weighing less than 10^{-12} grams, each is in effect a veritable micro-miniaturized factory containing thousands of exquisitely designed pieces of intricate molecular machinery, made up altogether of one hundred thousand million atoms, far more complicated than any machine built by man and absolutely without parallel in the non-living world.'[68]

Sir Julian Huxley, who claimed that evolution ran all the way 'from cosmic star-dust to human society',[69] blithely told the *News Chronicle* in 1950, 'There is every reason to believe that living matter developed automatically out of non-living matter in certain peculiar conditions of earth's early history',[70] but far from having 'every reason', we have none. We have no evidence that the random flow of energy through chemical 'soup' can lead to the staggering complexity of even the simplest living organism and no knowledge of any mechanism by which this could have been accomplished.

The renowned biochemist Professor Kause Dose, President of the Institute of Biochemistry at Germany's Johannes Gutenberg University, replaces fantasy with fact: 'More than thirty years of experimentation on the origin of life in the fields of chemical and molecular evolution have led to a better perception of the immensity of the problem of the origin of life on earth, rather than to its solution. At present all discussions on principal theories and experiments in the field either end in stalemate or in a confession of ignorance.'[71]

Hard-line evolutionists often say that the problem could be solved by factoring in a sufficient amount of time. As one scientist claimed, 'Time is the hero of the plot. Given enough time, anything can happen — the impossible becomes probable, the improbable becomes certain.'[72] But this escape route turns out to be a dead end. Writing in *Nature* magazine, Utah State University scholar Frank Salisbury discussed the odds against the spontaneous production of a single gene. He asked his readers to imagine one hundred million trillion planets, each with an ocean two kilometres deep and fairly rich in gene-sized DNA fragments, which reproduce one million times per second, with a mutation occurring at each reproduction. Under such favourable conditions, Salisbury calculated that it would take trillions of universes to have much chance of producing a single gene in four billion years — even if 10^{100} different DNA molecules could serve the same gene function![73]

The problem of explaining the origin of life became even greater in 1953 when the British biophysicist Francis Crick and his colleague James Watson discovered the now famous double-helical structure of DNA. Although it is a relatively simple molecule, with just four basic components, it governs all biological reproduction and the transmission of all inherited characteristics. The problem for the evolutionist is that, although DNA does this by *processing* an immense amount of genetic information, it does not *produce* it: 'The DNA molecule is the medium; it's not the message.'[74] This means that macro-evolution has to explain not only the origin of matter, but the independent origin of information, *without intelligence being a part of the equation.* Phillip Johnson illustrates this by saying that if all of Shakespeare's plays were destroyed, nothing would be permanently lost, as actors who had learned the roles could re-create the texts from memory. As Johnson goes on to say, 'This tells us that information is an entirely different kind of stuff from the physical medium in which it may temporarily be recorded.'[75] There is a lot of this 'stuff'! The chemical instructions for the construction of a complete human being exist in every fertilized human egg, and a single chromosome may contain information equivalent to 500 million words.[76] At 400 words to a page, it would take nearly 5,000 books of 230 pages to record it all — and a library of about 250,000 such books to store all the information secreted in the forty-six chromosomes in a single fertilized human egg. As if this were not amazing enough, all this information is encoded in a 'language' that has only four 'letters' and whose dictionary contains only sixty-four three-letter words. Where does this staggering mass of information come from? There is no known law of physics that could spontaneously create information and no example of information arising as the result of a mindless natural process. Dr Werner Gitt, Head of the Department of Technology at the German Federal Institute of Physics and Technology, confirms this: 'There is no known natural law through which matter can give rise to information, neither is there any physical process or material phenomenon known that can do this.'[77] As our common experience tells us that information always has an intelligent source, it is hardly surprising to find Stephen Grocott, Fellow of the Royal Australian Chemical Institute, concluding, 'I am afraid that as a scientist I simply cannot say strongly enough that spontaneous generation of life is a chemical nonsense and, therefore, I am left with no alternative but to believe that life was created.'[78]

Yet evolutionists continue to search for this most elusive of 'missing links', encouraged by knowing that living and non-living molecules are made up of exactly the same atoms (oxygen, hydrogen, carbon, sulphur and the like) and that under the right conditions small molecules can be made to combine to form larger and more complex ones. What eludes science is how, even given countless millions of years, simple, non-living molecules could have accidentally combined to produce those carrying the first spark of life. Dr Arthur Wilder-Smith, who earned three doctorates in organic chemistry and pharmacological sciences and held professorships at universities in the United States, Norway, Switzerland and Turkey (as well as becoming a three-star NATO general), had no hesitation in ruling out such a scenario: 'The evolutionary model says that it's not necessary to assume the existence of anything, besides matter and energy, to produce life. *That proposition is unscientific.* We know perfectly well that if you leave matter to itself it does not organize itself — in spite of all the efforts in recent years to prove that it does.'[79]

Out of nothing?

This has necessarily been a long chapter, but one last point needs to be squeezed in: where did material reality come from in the first place? We have tracked evolutionism back to an updated version of Darwin's 'warm little pond' — but where did the 'pond' come from? It is impossible to run any scientific programme that will show us how the universe began, but there seem to be just three possibilities: it is eternal; it was self-created; or it was brought into existence by a transcendent reality.

As far as the first possibility is concerned, Einstein's general theory of relativity, the First and Second Laws of Thermodynamics and numerous astronomical observations all point to a universe that is not eternal and static, but to one that had a definite beginning and is changing over time. According to Paul Davies, 'The most important discovery of our age is that the universe did not always exist.'[80]

The second possibility, that the universe is self-created, also collides with the Laws of Thermodynamics. In the simplest language possible, the First Law says that no new energy or matter can come into being, and none can be annihilated; applied in simple terms the Second Law says that the universe is like a clock that has been wound up and is now running down, becoming more and more randomized (disorganized) in the process.

This leaves just one alternative — that the universe was brought into being by a reality beyond it and greater than it. When there is no natural explanation for the existence of such a reality, should we not look for another one? Isaac Newton was convinced that the cosmos 'could only proceed from the counsel and dominion of an intelligent and powerful Being',[81] and Edgar Andrews calls this argument 'as close to a proof for the existence of God as is possible'.[82] It has been said that in order to have the universe as we know it, five basic things are needed — space, energy, matter, time and intelligence. All five concepts are contained in the Bible's opening words: 'In the beginning God created the heavens and the earth.'[83] Small wonder that the universally respected scholar C. S. Lewis said he had never come across any philosophical theory about origins that was 'a radical improvement' on these words.[84]

5.
Faith and facts

Present people with the words 'faith', 'science', 'facts' and 'religion', and ask them to arrange these in matching pairs, and many would have no hesitation in linking 'science' with 'facts' and 'religion' with 'faith'. Some have done this with passion. The British biologist T. H. Huxley, who invented the word 'agnostic' and became known as 'Darwin's Bulldog' because of his passionate promotion of Darwinism, once wrote that faith was no longer in contact with facts of any kind. Speaking at the 1992 Festival of Science in Edinburgh, Richard Dawkins said, 'Faith is the great cop-out, the great excuse to avoid the need to think and evaluate evidence … faith is not allowed to justify itself by argument.' When accepting the 1996 Humanist of the Year Award from the American Humanist Association, he made his point even more trenchantly: 'I think that a case can be made that faith is one of the world's great evils, comparable to the smallpox virus, but harder to eradicate. Faith, being belief that isn't based on evidence, is the principal vice of any religion.'[1]

This line has been so persistently promulgated that when seeking for solutions to life's problems many people look instinctively to science rather than to God. The story is told of the captain of a long-haul commercial flight announcing to the passengers: 'Ladies and gentlemen, I need to tell you that one of our engines has shut down, but please don't be concerned, because we still have three engines left and they can get us there without any difficulty. If any of you are still worried, let me tell you some good news. We have four bishops on board, so we are bound to be fine.' At this, a passenger called one of the cabin staff and said, 'Please tell the captain that I would be a lot happier if we had three bishops and four engines'!

Science: the faith factor

We hardly need to spend time proving that facts are the raw materials that fuel all science. They are the elements that science discovers and studies, then uses to make further progress in the endless search for truth in the natural world. The point we need to discuss is whether science is a discipline involving faith. In his acceptance speech quoted above, Richard Dawkins went on to say that, in his view, 'Science is free of the main vice of religion, which is faith.' However, there are highly qualified scientists who would say that this combines a wrong presumption (that faith is a vice) and a wrong conclusion (that science has none of it). Focusing on the subject of evolution, the American scientist Harold Urey, whose discovery of heavy hydrogen won him the 1934 Nobel Prize in chemistry, was committed to a materialistic world-view that had no place for God, yet he admitted, 'All of us who study the origin of life find that the more we look into it, the more we feel it is too complex to have evolved anywhere. We all believe *as an article of faith* that life evolved from dead matter on this planet.'[2] The American philosopher Marjorie Grene, a distinguished historian of science, wrote, 'It is as *a religion of science* that Darwinianism chiefly held, and holds man's minds... [It is] preached by its adherents with religious fervour.'[3]

As we saw in chapter 2, nobody is a 'non-believer'. The position of scientists who claim to have no faith in the God revealed in the Bible (or in any other god, for that matter) is not one that is devoid of faith, but one governed by the very principle they claim to despise. Atheists may claim that their view of the universe's origin, existence and nature is exclusively based on scientific facts, but the truth is that they lean heavily on the principle of faith. As we can easily show, every scientist acts on basic assumptions that cannot be logically or scientifically proved.

Assumptions

In the first place, scientists obviously assume *the reality and integrity of their own existence*. In the seventeenth century the French mathematician René Descartes was deeply concerned that established belief systems were being challenged by new scientific discoveries. In an attempt to hold them together, he tried to bring certainty into philosophy by setting aside everything that could possibly be doubted in order to find something that was beyond *all* doubt. It was one thing for science to claim that we should rely on our senses — but how could we know that they were reliable? After a great deal of tortuous mental wrestling he coined the phrase for which he is now most famous: '*Cogito, ergo sum*' ('I think, therefore I am'). Descartes used his doubts to confirm that he must exist as a thinking, doubting being. He was eventually to push his ideas so far that he became known as one of the fathers of modern rationalism, which says that reason alone is the primary source of all human knowledge and is sufficient to solve all the problems of man's nature and destiny. It is not difficult to dismantle this, but no scientist will make any progress at all until he or she accepts Descartes' most famous dictum.

In the second place, scientists assume that *the universe exists as an objective, independent reality outside of themselves*. This assumption goes back at least as far as ancient Greek thinkers such as Plato, Aristotle and Socrates (even though some of them thought the universe not worthy of study) and is so fundamental that without it science would not merely grind to a halt; it could never get started in the first place. Yet as Del Ratzsch points out, the universe's existence is exactly what one would expect 'if the nature [that] science studies were a creation'.[4]

Thirdly, scientists assume that *nature is uniform* — that what we have around us is cosmos, not chaos. We have seen only a microscopic part of all natural reality, and have only done so for a tiny amount of time, but we assume that the reality around us is regular in its behaviour, so that we can record its details and work on understanding something of what it means. If we did not assume that processes and patterns in nature were universally consistent, we could never be sure that the laws of nature would work the same way tomorrow as they do today. Yet there is no logical reason why they should. The fact that the sun has risen every day of your life is no logical guarantee that it will rise tomorrow. In Albert Einstein's famous phrase, 'The most incomprehensible fact of nature is that it is comprehensible.'[5]

Science can only proceed at all on the assumption that the world is orderly and predictable. If the law of gravity suddenly went into reverse so that apples shaken loose by the wind fell upwards instead of downwards, not only scientists would find life difficult and revise the way they act! Paul Davies has no hesitation in conceding what this means: 'You have to accept as an act of faith that there is an existing order in nature that is intelligible to us. That is a huge act of faith.'[6]

Fourthly, scientists in every discipline assume that *their senses enable them to discover accurate data about nature and to communicate true information to others.* In other words, they trust that their senses are telling them the truth because they are in some way 'logged on' to the world around them. As two modern professors of science put it, 'It is a striking and non-trivial fact that the pattern of mathematics is realized in the physical structure of the world and that our minds are able to solve problems that the physical world presents.'[7]

Fifthly, scientists assume *the law of cause and effect*. The entire scientific enterprise is built on the premise that within an ordered world effects must be related to causes. The noted entomologist Stanley Beck, although strongly opposed to the concept of divine creation, conceded, 'The ... best-known postulate underlying the structure of scientific knowledge is that of cause and effect.'[8] Scientists have an inbuilt conviction that every event can be explained as the product of some previous event.

Sixthly, scientists believe that *things they can see give clues to things they cannot see*. Del Ratzsch gives an obvious example: 'We cannot directly see atoms and other such micro-entities, yet most scientists are confident of their existence on the basis of large-scale things that human eyes can see — cloud-chamber tracks and so forth. On the other end of the scale are phenomena that scientists are confident about but which are simply too big for humans to see. Scientists talk confidently about the large-scale structure of the universe and about the long-term history or future of the universe. We cannot directly follow such processes on our small temporal and spatial scale of observation, but what we can see is taken as evidence for such processes.'[9]

These six fundamental assumptions knock huge holes in the Dawkins dogma that science is free from the 'vice' of faith. Without faith (in the sense of assuming things that cannot be logically proven) science would never get off the ground. All scientists are deeply committed to the principle of faith: they assume their own integrity, the existence of the world as an objective reality, the uniformity of nature, the dependability of their senses, the law of cause and effect and the existence of reality beyond their physical sight. To put it simply, every scientist exercises faith while searching for facts.

Interestingly, all of these assumptions fit perfectly into a biblical, theistic world-view. The first two are perfectly covered by the statement that God 'made heaven and earth and sea and everything in them'. [10] A biblical view of nature, with God as its Creator, offers a credible explanation of the third assumption, which concerns balance and elegance of natural law. Theologian Elaine Storkey, Senior Research Fellow at Wycliffe Hall, Oxford, rightly told *Soul of Britain*, 'The reason science is possible is that we live in a law-ordered cosmos which God has created.'[11] Del Ratzsch underlines the point: 'Uniformity is what we would expect of a creation that is established by a God who is faithful and that is governed by his edicts.'[12] The biblical claim that there is a common Creator of both material and mind goes hand in glove with the fourth assumption, that our senses enable us to 'log on' to the world around us. The fifth, an elegant link between cause and effect, is what we would expect from a Creator whose own character is orderly and consistent. Finally, an amazing cosmos, most of which is beyond the limits of our physical vision, is entirely consistent with its being the work of a transcendent Creator whose greatness 'no one can fathom'[13] and whose ways are 'beyond tracing out'.[14]

At the end of the day, science of any kind is a discipline essentially based on faith. Without the assumption of order in the universe, science could never get started, let alone come to any solid conclusions about anything. Although not a professing Christian, Albert Einstein wrote, 'To the sphere of religion belongs the faith that the regulations valid for the world of existence are rational, that it is comprehensible to reason. I cannot conceive of a genuine scientist without that profound faith.'[15] The world-class scientist Sir John Polkinghorne agrees: 'In every true searcher of Nature there is a kind of religious reverence; for he finds it impossible to imagine that he is first to have thought out the exceedingly delicate threads that connect his perceptions. The aspect of knowledge which has not yet been laid bare gives the investigator a feeling akin to that of a child who seeks to grasp the masterly way in which elders manipulate things.'[16] Small wonder that the German physicist Max Planck, who won the Nobel prize for Physics in 1918 and considered the search for universal laws of physics 'the most

sublime scientific pursuit in life', made this categorical declaration: 'Anybody who has seriously engaged in scientific work of
any kind realizes that over the gates of the temple of science are
written the words, "You must have faith." It is a quality which
the scientist cannot dispense with.'[17]

Stephen Barr sums it up very well: 'So we see in science
something akin to religious faith. The scientist has confidence in
the intelligibility of the world. He has questions about nature.
And he expects — no, more than expects, he is absolutely
convinced — that these questions have intelligible answers. The
fact that he must seek those answers proves that they are not in
sight. The fact that he continues to seek them in spite of all
difficulties testifies to his unconquerable conviction that those
answers, although not presently in sight, do in fact exist. Truly,
the scientist too walks by faith and not by sight.'[18]

Scientists who accept the truth of these assumptions, but
who reject the idea that they are signs of science pointing
beyond itself to a transcendent God, run headlong into a thicket
of even greater mysteries. The contemporary British author and
one-time atheist Dr Rob Frost points out some of these: 'If the
scientist prefers to suggest that there is no "God", no "Creator",
and no "first cause", what does atheism offer him intellectually?
The atheist must, of necessity, believe that matter without mind
created reason and logic. Matter without intelligence created
understanding and comprehension. Matter without morals
created complex ethical codes and legal systems. Matter without
conscience created a sense of right and wrong. Matter without
emotion created skills and art, music, drama, architecture,
comedy, literature and dance. Matter without design created in
humankind an insatiable hunger for meaning and purpose.'[19]

Basis of faith

Nothing I have written in this chapter (or in the rest of the book)
is meant to suggest that there are not superb and even world-

class scientists who are atheists or agnostics. In addition, there are doubtless equally distinguished scientists who are Jews, Muslims, Hindus or Buddhists, or who subscribe to one of a multitude of other faith systems. One religious organization even has a title — Christian Science — that seems to suggest that it is the definitive way of welding science and Christian faith together. But there is more (or less!) to this title than meets the eye and rather than interrupt the flow of this chapter I have examined Christian Science in an appendix. Our focus here is on mainstream Christianity and the relationship between facts and faith.

When concentrating on science, we noted that it was fuelled by facts and that the point at issue was whether faith was involved. In concentrating on Christianity, we can obviously turn the coin over and take the issue of faith for granted. The question we need to tackle is whether biblical faith can be justified on any factual basis.

We can get right to the heart of the matter by looking at what is seen by many people to be one of Christianity's greatest weaknesses, the biblical accounts of miracles. The eighteenth-century Scottish thinker David Hume was so sceptical on the subject that he felt the only genuine miracle was that people believed in miracles at all! Yet whatever reason might be advanced for rejecting the possibility of miracles, it is impossible to reject them on *scientific* grounds. In *Quarks, Chaos and Christianity,* Sir John Polkinghorne writes, 'The question of miracles is not primarily scientific, but *theological.* Science simply tells us that these events are against normal expectation. We knew this from the start. *Science cannot exclude the possibility that, on particular occasions, God does particular, unprecedented things.* After all, he is the ordainer of the laws of nature, not someone who is subject to them.' [20]

The laws of nature are merely our assessment of how God normally causes things to happen. But he is not subject to those laws and is at perfect liberty to suspend or change them on a local or more widespread basis whenever and for whatever reason he chooses; nor would his doing so violate any known law. If in the course of setting the table for a meal my wife dropped a knife it would normally fall to the ground, but if I was quick-fingered enough to catch it before it hit the floor I would not be breaking any law of physics, merely intervening. If this is true at a purely human level, it is certainly true at a divine level, and science is unable to prove that such a thing never happens. In a letter to *The Times* in 1984, thirteen prominent scientists, most of them university professors, clinically closed this particular door: 'It is not logically valid to use science as an argument against miracles. To believe that miracles cannot happen is as much an act of faith as to believe that they can happen ... miracles are unprecedented events. Whatever the current fashions in philosophy or the revelations of opinion polls may suggest, *it is important to affirm that science ... can have nothing to say on the subject.*'[21]

The only sensible way to tackle the issue is to do so openly and honestly. As historian Philip Schaff says, 'The purpose of the historian is not to construct a history from preconceived notions and to adjust it to his own liking, but to reproduce it from the best evidence and let it speak for itself.'[22] For anyone to reject miracles not on strictly scientific grounds but because they clash with his or her world-view is to evade the issue instead of examining it. The right approach is to look at the data with an open mind, ask the right questions, examine all the evidence as closely as possible, and then come to a clear conclusion as to where it points. This approach should begin by accepting that if God is personal and wants to communicate with us, it is at least possible that from time to time he might choose to do so in unusual or even unique ways. Ruling God out from the start is to feed false criteria into the whole business; to deny miracles because they are beyond human explanation is both arrogant and foolish. As the nineteenth-century British author Charles Caleb Colson teased, 'He who believes only what he can comprehend must have a very long head or a very short creed.'[23] The only way to know whether miracles *can* occur is to see whether any *have* occurred. The Bible gives us a perfect opportunity to pursue the point.

A test case

In the course of an address at the University of Cape Town I was heckled by a militant atheist and after the meeting I had a long discussion with him about the existence of God. Needing to leave for another engagement, I asked him one last question: 'What do you think of Jesus?' His immediate reply was, 'I don't know — but I do realize that everything hinges on whether he rose again from the dead.' He was absolutely right! Christianity stands or falls by this one event, because it pins all the others in place. The Bible says that in rising from the dead Jesus was 'declared with power to be the Son of God'[24] and an amplified version of the original Greek text brings out the force of what is being said: '[He was] openly designated the Son of God in power — in a striking, triumphant and miraculous manner.'[25] In simple terms, the resurrection is said to be a declaration of his deity.

The background can be sketched in very quickly. After being betrayed by Judas Iscariot and tortured by his captors, Jesus was shuttled from one show trial to another, before being put to death by crucifixion just outside Jerusalem. A wealthy follower obtained permission to remove the body and bury it in his own private tomb, carved out of a rock in a nearby garden. There were several witnesses to the burial. Because of the controversy surrounding the trial and execution of Jesus, a detachment of soldiers was posted at the tomb and the Roman governor's official seal was attached to a huge rock placed over the entrance.

Three days later there was the first-century equivalent of a modern media frenzy: *the body was missing!* This was confirmed by at least five people who visited the site on the day the story broke — and nobody ever contradicted their testimony.

An empty tomb falls a long way short of proof that Jesus had come back from the dead, but soon afterwards (and for the rest of their lives) his followers openly preached that he had. All the authorities had to do to prove them lunatics or liars was to open the tomb for public inspection, and the fact that they did no such thing is hugely significant. As the German theologian Paul Althaus rightly said, 'The resurrection proclamation could not have been maintained in Jerusalem for a single day, for a single hour, if the emptiness of the tomb had not been established as a fact for all concerned.'[26]

Some objections answered

Sceptics have always recognized the significance of the resurrection, and over the centuries have come up with a barrage of alternative explanations for the missing body. Here are some of them:

Jesus never died. The so-called 'swoon theory' was popularized in the eighteenth century, but it is a non-starter. Even before his crucifixion, Jesus had been viciously beaten and scourged, while on the cross his body was ripped open by a soldier's spear for the express purpose of confirming his death.[27] At no time during his body's removal and burial did any of its handlers detect the slightest sign of life. Yet the swoon theory asks us to believe that in the stone-cold tomb Jesus came out of a coma, wriggled his way out of tightly-wound grave-clothes layered with sticky, hardening embalming material weighing seventy-five pounds,[28] pushed aside the massive rock lying across the tomb, overcame an armed guard of Roman soldiers, went back into the city stark naked (or clutching some of the grave-clothes) and then convinced his friends, not that he had had a near-death experience, but that he had actually died, then overcome death for ever. Small wonder that even a hardened sceptic like the nineteenth-century German scholar David Strauss dismissed the swoon theory as 'impossible'![29]

The first visitors all went to the wrong tomb. This idea was first suggested in 1907, but it should have died at birth. Two of these visitors had not only been present at the burial but had even noticed 'how his body was laid in it'[30] — and in any case, would the owner of the tomb he had originally chosen for himself have forgotten where it was?

The body was stolen by a person or persons unknown. This scenario is devoid of evidence, opportunity or motive. As Sir Norman Anderson, one-time Director of the Institute of Advanced Legal Studies in the University of London, wryly says, 'A Jew of that period could scarcely be suspected of stealing bodies on behalf of anatomical research.'[31]

The Roman authorities stole the body. They would obviously have had the best opportunity, but no conceivable motive. Their whole purpose in posting an armed guard was *to keep the body where it was.*

The Jewish authorities removed the body. They shared the Roman authorities' interest in keeping the body secure for four days (taking it beyond the 'third day', when Jesus had prophesied that he would rise again) but why should their custody be thought any more secure than that of the Romans, which was backed up by armed force? When Jesus' followers began preaching that Jesus was alive again they were arrested, flogged, imprisoned and assassinated — all totally unnecessary if the Jewish authorities had produced the body. As the nineteenth-century Scottish theologian Professor Andrew Fairbairn noted, 'The silence of the Jews is as significant as the speech of the Christians.'[32]

Jesus' disciples removed the body. This story did the rounds at the time, but we are told that it was deliberately invented by the Jewish authorities to discredit the disciples. Besides, how would a few terrified followers have been able to overcome the Roman guards? Why would they risk their own lives by breaking the governor's official seal? Why move a body already in the safe keeping of one of their own number? Why is there no record of their ever being charged with grave robbery? Why put their lives on the line by preaching that they had seen Jesus alive, when they had his body hidden somewhere? They might have risked their lives for something they imagined, but not for something they had invented.

Charles Colson, one of United States President Richard Nixon's advisers at the time of the Watergate scandal that ended his presidency in the 1970s, tells how, within a month, three of those involved in the notorious burglary had gone to the Department of Justice to turn state evidence. Commenting on this some time later Colson wrote, 'In my Watergate experience I saw the inability of men — powerful, highly motivated professionals — to hold together a conspiracy based on a lie... Yet Christ's followers maintained to their grim deaths by execution that they had in fact seen Jesus Christ raised from the dead. There was no conspiracy... Men and women do not give up their comfort — and certainly not their lives — for what they know to be a lie.'[33]

Sir Norman Anderson claims that the disciples' transformation from cowardice to courage is 'far and away the strongest circumstantial evidence for the resurrection'.[34]

There is more...

But we can go beyond circumstantial evidence. There are six independent written testimonies, three of them by eyewitnesses, of Jesus having appeared alive after his dead body had been in the tomb for three days. These record eleven separate appearances over a period of forty days,[35] with over 500 people present on one particular occasion.[36] Sceptics suggest that these reports can be written off as hallucinations, but the appearances fail to conform to any of the known laws relating to the subject. There is no evidence that any of the witnesses were neurotic or psychotic, and Jesus rarely appeared in places where he and his followers had spent time together. What is more, resurrection was the last thing his followers expected. They were utterly demoralized and quite certain that Jesus was dead and buried. His resurrection came as a shock to them, rather than as wish-fulfilment; several did not believe it when they were first told[37] and others were alarmed.[38] After considering all the issues involved, the eminent surgeon Arthur Rendle Short concluded, 'The resurrection appearances break every known law of visions.'[39]

Some 2,000 years on, those claiming to be Christians form the largest religious group the world has ever known, and its origin is to be found, not in its style of worship, nor in any particular stance on social issues, nor in a new line of moral philosophy, but in one single event: *the resurrection of Jesus from the dead.* As the American author D. James Kennedy says, 'The Grand Canyon wasn't caused by an Indian dragging a stick, and the Christian Church wasn't created by a myth.'[40]

Others have added more formal endorsements. The seventeenth-century Dutch jurist and humanist Hugo Grotius, who came to be known as 'the father of international law', strongly defended the historical fact of Jesus' resurrection in his book *The Truth of the Christian Religion.* In the eighteenth century, Lord Lyndhurst was in turn Solicitor General, Attorney General, Master of the Rolls and Lord Chancellor of England. When he died in 1863, his obituary in *The Times* said of him, 'No man was more free from corrupt notions or acted more independently of sordid influence.' Lord Lyndhurst's assessment of the resurrection narrative was as follows: 'I know pretty well what evidence is; and I tell you, such evidence as that for the resurrection has never broken down yet.'[41] Dr Simon Greenleaf, Dane Professor of Law at Harvard University, has been considered 'the greatest single authority on evidence in the entire literature on legal procedure'.[42] He once wrote that if the testimony of witnesses to the resurrection of Jesus were to be sifted 'as if it were in a court of law, on the side of the adverse party, the witnesses being subjected to a rigorous cross-examination', the result, 'it is confidently believed, will be an undoubting conviction of their integrity, ability and truth'.[43] Lord Caldecote, Lord Chief Justice of England, said that an 'over-whelming case' could be made for the resurrection 'merely as a matter of strict evidence'.[44] Lord Darling, who also served as Lord Chief Justice of England, concluded, 'There exists such overwhelming evidence, positive and negative, that no intelligent jury in the world could fail to bring in a verdict that the resurrection story is true.'[45]

Implications

There are far-reaching implications here, both negative and positive.

If Christ did not rise

If Jesus did not rise from the dead, he himself was either deluded or dishonest (as he said that he would rise) and the early disciples were a rabble of blasphemous deceivers. What is more, all the Christian martyrs down the centuries (and there have been millions of them) have spilt their blood for something that never happened; Christian reformers of society have been motivated by a pack of lies; every Christian church building is a monument to a myth; every service held in them is a pointless farce; and Easter Day commemorates a non-event.

But if he did...

The positive implications are even greater. Jesus clearly stated that God is the Creator of all other reality.[46] He specifically underlined the Old Testament's pivotal creed that God is uniquely and peerlessly sovereign over all of his creation.[47] He fully endorsed the integrity and divine authority of the Old

Testament.[48] He confirmed the historicity of events recorded there, including those most often questioned by sceptics.[49] He underlined the God-given authority of the Old Testament prophets.[50] He uniquely claimed to be the fulfilment of all the prophecies about a coming Messiah.[51] He repeatedly taught that every person who ever lived would be morally and spiritually accountable to God on a coming day of final judgement.[52]

This helps to make another tremendously important point, which is that any discussion about the integrity, accuracy, inerrancy or authority of the Bible is directly tied in to the resurrection of Jesus from the dead. His resurrection confirms his deity; his deity guarantees the truth of his teaching; and his teaching establishes Scripture as being 'the living and enduring word of God'.[53] The linkage is clear.

T. H. Huxley's statement that faith is no longer in contact with facts of any kind is worse than threadbare, and for Richard Dawkins to claim that science is free of the 'vice' of faith is to replace reality with rhetoric. True science and true biblical religion both involve faith as well as facts, and they are not antagonists, but allies, combining to give us a true picture of reality.

The British physicist William Henry Bragg was the senior member of a unique team when in 1915 he and his son William Lawrence Bragg won the Nobel Prize for physics for their seminal work in X-ray crystallography. In a lecture at the Royal Institution in London four years later he stated, 'Sometimes people ask if religion and science are opposed to each other. They are — in the sense that the thumb and fingers of my hand are opposed to each other. It is an opposition by means of which anything can be grasped.'

Albert Einstein used another vivid metaphor to say the same thing: 'A legitimate conflict between science and religion cannot exist. Science without religion is lame; religion without science is blind.'[54]

6.
Lazy fatheads?

In sending centenary greetings to the Rational Press Association, Peter Atkins drew a distinction between what he called a rational (scientific) and an irrational (religious) search for truth and claimed that the latter led the 'false-footed' to 'sink into the feigned comfort of fraudulent expectations and self-deception masquerading as an understanding'.[1] In an article for *Free Inquiry Magazine* he warmed to his subject: 'Science respects the power of the human intellect; religion belittles it… Science is progressively advancing toward complete knowledge, leaving religions bobbing about in its wake… Religion is armchair speculation well fitted to adipose brains.'[2] In the course of the 1998 Oxford debate referred to earlier in this book he called religion 'outmoded and ridiculous' and claimed that it was 'not possible to believe in gods and be a true scientist'.[3] This hardly leaves us in any doubt as to where he is coming from, and in a review of *Darwin's Black Box* he sharpened his attack by calling God 'this incompetent figment of impoverished imaginations'.[4]

These are serious accusations, and if Atkins is right the only sensible way to search for truth is to reject any idea of God and concentrate on an approach driven by scientific rationalism — *but is he right?* The first indication that he is not comes when we compare the results of two polls of scientists taken in the United States over a time-span of eighty years. The first was taken in 1914 by the American academic

James Leuba and showed that about 40% of those interviewed said they believed in God.[5] The second, geared to
replicate Leuba's approach, was conducted by *Nature* in
1996 and produced almost identical results.[6] Commenting on
the 1996 survey, Peter Atkins still held to his core claim: 'You
can clearly be a scientist and have religious beliefs. But I don't
think you can be a real scientist in the deepest sense of the
word.'[7]

This seems totally at odds with the fact that the study of
the relationship between science and theology is one of the
fastest-growing academic areas in the world, with organizations of scientists committed to belief in God flourishing on
an unprecedented scale. In the United States, the American
Scientific Affiliation has some 2,500 members drawn from
most of the nation's fifty states and some forty other coun-
tries. Also based in the United States, the Creation Research
Society, committed to a biblical world-view, has an international membership of about 1,750, with all its voting
members having at least one earned postgraduate degree in a
recognized area of science. In Britain, over 5,000 doctors are
members of the Christian Medical Fellowship, which also has
1,000 student members and active links with some sixty
similar organizations worldwide. Also based in Britain, Christians in Science has over 600 members, including several
distinguished senior scientists. Over 150 Ph.D. scientists and
300 other scientists with masters' degrees are members of the
Korea Association of Creation Research, whose aim is 'to see
science return to its rightful, God-glorying position'. Listing
the many like-minded organizations flourishing on all five
continents, whose members are committed believers in
specialized fields from astronomy to zoology, would take up
too much space in a book of this size, but their sheer numbers
and quality would seem to be *prima facie* evidence against
Peter Atkins's claim that it is impossible to be 'a true scientist'
(or 'a real scientist') and believe in God.

History says…

His claim also sits awkwardly with any honest examination of the rise of modern science. Although the term 'scientist' was not used until 1834, concepts such as the argument from design (i.e., the universe shows evidence of design, so there must be a Designer) go back thousands of years. The Bible lays down some very clear principles here. To quote just one example, an Old Testament writer addresses God in these words:

> In the beginning you laid the foundations of the earth,
>   and the heavens are the work of your hands.
> They will perish, but you remain;
>   they will wear out like a garment.
> Like clothing you will change them
>   and they will be discarded.
> But you remain the same,
>   and your years will never end.[8]

Science as we now know it came into existence in the sixteenth and seventeenth centuries, and it did so in a God-centred culture, driven by the biblical conviction that nature has a divine and eternal Creator upon whom it is totally dependent. This was vastly different from a pagan world-view, with its exotic assortment of deities, including the sun, moon and stars, who were themselves part of the material universe. As Reijer Hooykaas, Professor of the History of Science at the University of Utrecht, pointed out, the biblical picture shows us that '… in total contradiction to pagan religion, nature is not a deity to be feared and worshipped, but a work of God to be admired, studied and managed.'[9]

U. S. News & World Report called Dr John Baumgardner 'the world's pre-eminent expert in the design of computer models for geophysical convection'.[10] His three-dimensional computer model for Earth's interior is recognized as the most capable computer model of its type in the world and NASA sees it as cutting-edge science in the field. In an interview given in 1997, Dr Baumgardner said, 'I believe science as we know it is a product of the Christian world-view. It was only in the Christian world that science was developed and I believe could have developed. For example, in the Buddhist or Hindu world-view this physical reality is more or less regarded as an illusion and not representing ultimate reality. Of course, Christians don't regard this world as eternal, but nevertheless it's real. Science has flowed from a Christian understanding of God, and a Christian understanding of the natural world.'[11]

Convictions like these fuelled the explosive launch of modern science. When the Royal Society, which claims to be the oldest learned society still in existence, came into being in 1660, its founders dedicated their work 'to the glory of God'. The manifesto of the British Association for the Advancement of Science, drawn up in 1865 and signed by 617 scientists, including many with outstanding credentials, expressed unambiguous belief in the truth and authority of the Bible and its harmony with natural sciences. These are two outstanding illustrations of the world-view that dominated the thrust of scientific thinking at that time. As the modern American author Henry Morris says, 'The most discerning historians and philosophers of science have recognized that the very existence of modern science had its origins in a culture at least nominally committed to a biblical basis, and at a time in history marked by a great return to biblical faith.'[12]

Hall of fame

Over the three-and-a-half centuries since then, countless scientists, over the complete range of scientific disciplines, have been committed to a world-view that sees an orderly universe obeying dependable laws put in place by a transcendent Creator who has revealed himself in the pages of the Bible.

Many of these people have made enormous and sometimes seminal contributions to their particular disciplines. Names and numbers are not in themselves any criteria of truth, nor should we rely on an accumulation of honours to prove a point, but there are sufficient examples to make nonsense of the claim that religion belittles the intellect. Science has seen so many God-fearing trailblazers that the problem is not knowing where to start, but when to stop. What follows is mainly a historical survey, but the status of the scientists concerned and the enduring quality of their work are beyond dispute. Taken together, the evidence makes it crystal clear that the very origins of modern scientific thinking were provided by men of faith who had a mindset that has largely been lost by many people currently involved in science. We shall take twelve of these giants as representatives of them all.

Although now most popularly known for his sublime paint-ings (even though he left behind only a handful of completed works) the Italian genius *Leonardo da Vinci* (1452-1519) was also 'an experimental scientist long before the formulation of the so-called scientific method'.[13] He left evidence of prolific work in subjects as diverse as dynamics, anatomy, physics, optics, biology, physiology, hydraulics, geometry, architecture, me-chanics and aeronautics, much of it far in advance of his time. Yet running parallel to this amazing diversity of talent was his devout belief in God and in Jesus Christ as the Saviour of the world, powerfully expressed in *The Last Supper*, his best-known work of art.

As we saw in chapter 3, the English philosopher, scientist and politician *Francis Bacon* (1561-1626) made an enormous contribution to science with his development of the inductive method, stressing the importance of observation and experi-ment. Bacon saw not the slightest conflict between the Bible and natural science: 'There are two books laid before us to study, to prevent our falling into error; first, the volume of the Scriptures, which reveal the will of God; then the volume of the Creatures, which expresses his power.'[14] This conviction stayed

with him throughout his extraordinary career and towards the
end of his life he wrote, 'Let no man think or maintain that a
man can search too far or be too well studied in the book of
God's word or in the book of God's works.'[15] In view of later
developments, it is ironic that Charles Darwin reproduced these
words on the flyleaf of *Origin*!

The German scientist *Johannes Kepler* (1571-1630) did
important work in optics, discovered two new regular polyhedra
(solid figures with many identical faces), gave the first proof of
how logarithms worked, calculated the precise astronomical
tables that helped to establish heliocentric astronomy and
contributed to the eventual discovery of calculus. He is best
remembered for discovering the three laws of planetary motion
that now bear his name. Subsequently called 'the first theoretical astrophysicist' and now universally acknowledged as the
father of physical astronomy, Kepler saw all his work as a
fulfilment of his Christian duty. He famously said that he was
only 'thinking God's thoughts after him', and once prayed, 'I
give you thanks, Creator and God, that you have given me this
joy in your creation, and I rejoice in the works of your hands.'
He once wrote, 'Since we astronomers are the priests of the
highest God in regard to the books of nature, it befits us to be
thoughtful, not of the glory of our minds, but rather, above all
else, the glory of God.'[16]

The French mathematician, philosopher and scientist *Blaise
Pascal* (1623-1662) can fairly be called a genius. At twelve
years of age he proved some of Euclid's theorems on his own.
By the time he was sixteen his book on conic sections was
acknowledged as the greatest advance in geometry since the
times of the ancient Greeks, and three years later he invented a
calculating machine. Later, he worked in the fields of atmos-
pheric and fluid mechanics, hydrostatics and mathematics.
Conclusions reached in tandem with the notable French
mathematician Pierre de Fermat formed the basis of modern
insurance and probability theory — and in a final flourish he
took the lead in establishing a public transport system for Paris!

As if this were not enough, his writings on other subjects were so outstanding that they were said to have 'elevated French prose to new heights of power and form'.[17] In all of this, Pascal's Christian faith was his dominant passion, leading him to write, 'Not only do we know God through Jesus Christ alone, but we do not even know ourselves except through Jesus Christ.'[18] He saw bringing glory to God as the sole purpose of all his life and work. Shortly before he died he prayed, 'Grant that I may conform to thy will, just as I am, that, sick as I am, I may glorify thee in my suffering.'[19]

The Irish chemist *Robert Boyle* (1627-1691) was the four-teenth child and last son of Richard Boyle, Earl of Cork, said to be the wealthiest man in the British Isles. Educated in England, France and Switzerland, Boyle developed a formidable repu-tation for his work in mechanics, medicine and hydrodynamics, but chemistry was his main interest, and his precision in defin-ing chemical elements and chemical reactions was a major step in separating the science of chemistry from alchemy, its medi-eval forerunner. He made a massive contribution to the devel-opment of modern chemical thought, his best-known legacy being Boyle's Law, which establishes the relationship between the pressure, temperature and volume of a mass of gas. Above all, Boyle was a committed Christian. He was so concerned to know and understand the Bible that in a single year he taught himself four languages in order to help him do so. He devoted time, energy — and a considerable amount of money — to having the Bible translated and distributed into Irish, Turkish and several native American languages. Far from finding that the Bible's teaching clashed with his scientific discoveries, he repeatedly claimed 'the truth of the history of the Scriptures'[20] and once wrote that 'the seeming contradictions betwixt Divin-ity and true philosophy' were few 'and the real ones none at all'.[21] As well as writing over forty books popularizing science, he intended to complete a major work countering atheism, but died before the manuscript was completed. Described on his tombstone as 'the father of chemistry', and one of the founders of the Royal Society, Boyle saw no contradiction between his science and his Christian faith. In his last message to the society he urged his fellow scientists, 'Remember to give glory to the one who authored nature.'[22]

One of Boyle's contemporaries was the English naturalist, philosopher and theologian *John Ray* (1627-1705). A Cambridge graduate, Ray became an expert in languages, mathematics and natural science and was the greatest authority of his day in both botany and zoology. As well as doing experiments in embryology and plant physiology (he was the first to prove that the wood of a living tree conducts water) he published systematic works on plants, birds, mammals, fish and insects, his plant classification becoming the first to divide flowering plants into monocotyledons and dicotyledons. Described in *The Dictionary of National Biography* as 'the father of English natural history', Ray was ordained as a Church of England minister as well as being inducted into the Royal Society in recognition of his outstanding scientific work. He saw no clash between the two positions. Late in life he wrote two major theological books, *The Wisdom of God Manifested in the Works of the Creation* and *Three Physico-Theological Discourses.* The first of these, translated into several foreign languages and reprinted for over fifty years, made his personal convictions clear: 'There is for a free man no occupation more worthy and delightful than to contemplate the beauteous works of nature and honour the infinite wisdom and goodness of God.'[23]

The English mathematician and philosopher *Sir Isaac Newton* (1642-1727) was a colossus of science who bestrode the seventeenth and eighteenth centuries and is generally recognized as one of the greatest scientists who ever lived. He is best known for his discovery of the law of universal gravitation (supposedly inspired by the sight of a falling apple), but he also formulated the three laws of motion which laid the groundwork for classical mechanics, developed the particle theory of light propagation, constructed the first reflecting telescope, lectured on optics, published a law of thermodynamics now known as 'Newton's Law of Cooling' and shared credit with the German mathematician and philosopher Gottfried Leibnitz for the development of differential calculus, now a basic scientific tool. A devout Bible student, he said, 'We account the Scriptures of God to be the most sublime philosophy. I find more sure marks of authenticity in the Bible than in any profane history whatsoever.'[24] In his greatest work, *Philosophiae Naturalis Principia Mathematica*, written to persuade people 'for the belief of a Deity', he said, 'Without all doubt this world ... could arise from nothing but the perfectly free will of God.'[25]

The Swedish scientist *Carolus Linneaus* (1707-1778) trained for the Christian ministry but was constantly being drawn in other directions. He studied medicine at the Universities of Lund and Uppsala but, although he practised medicine for several years, and eventually became Professor of Medicine at Uppsala, he could not escape a consuming interest in botany. His greatest longing was to produce a detailed classification system of plants and animals, and he went to extraordinary lengths to draw this up. Although his intention to classify every living species in the entire world was obviously beyond him, his achievements were such that he has become known as the father of biological taxonomy. The Linnean Society of London, founded in his honour, became the focal gathering point for the leading naturalists of the nineteenth century, and his system of classification is still in standard use today. Linneaus was a firm believer in special creation and the fixity of species and his works teem with references to God. He once wrote, 'One is completely stunned by the incredible resourcefulness of the Creator... I followed his footsteps over nature's field and saw everywhere an eternal wisdom and power, an inscrutable perfection.'[26]

Moving on ...

The English chemist and physicist *Michael Faraday* (1791-1867) takes us into the nineteenth century and was another scientist with a prolific output. Though he seems to have had little or no formal education, he was a voracious reader of scientific literature and was eventually to discover electromagnetic induction (which opened the way for the generation and industrial use of electricity), the magneto-optical effect, diamagnetism and field theory. The foremost experimental scientist of his day, he also introduced the concept of magnetic lines of force, invented the dynamo and formulated the second law of electrolysis. Elected to the Royal Society and eventually awarded the society's Royal and Rumford medals, Faraday stands as a giant in his field, and today two basic units, one in electrolysis (the faraday) and one in electrostatics (the farad), are named in his honour. He was not without a sense of humour. Legend has it that he tried to explain one of his inventions to the Prime Minister or Chancellor of the Exchequer. On being asked, 'But what use is it?', Faraday is said to have replied, 'Why sir, there is the probability that you will soon be able to tax it!' Although a towering force in his fields of expertise, Faraday's strong Christian faith was reflected in his humility and he declined both a knighthood and the presidency of the Royal Society, feeling that these were inappropriate honours for a follower of Christ. He preached regularly in his church and subscribed wholeheartedly to its basis of faith, which included the statement: 'The Bible, and it alone, with nothing added to it, nor taken away from it by man, is the sole and sufficient guide for each individual, at all times and in all circumstances.'[27] It is said that in reply to someone who asked him on his deathbed what his speculations were, Faraday testified to his faith in God by replying, 'Speculations? I have none. I am relying on certainties.'

The first of our examples to be born in the nineteenth century was the English physicist *James Joule* (1818-1889).

Afflicted with a spinal disorder from his early days, he was educated at home until he was fifteen, though for three years after that he and his older brother were taught chemistry, physics, the scientific method and mathematics by the outstanding English chemist John Dalton, the founder of modern atomic theory. Joule was fascinated by the relationship between heat, electricity and mechanical work, and in 1839 he submitted a paper — 'On the Production of Heat by Voltaic Electricity' — to the Royal Society. His work got a cool reception from the society and elsewhere, largely because scientists were reluctant to accept the extreme accuracy of his measurements. Two notable exceptions to this scepticism were William Thomson (see below) and Michael Faraday. With their encouragement Joule submitted a further paper — 'On the Mechanical Equivalent of Heat' — to the Royal Society in 1849. The society not only published the paper, but elected him a member and later honoured him with the Copley Medal, its oldest and highest award. He was twice elected President of the British Association for the Advancement of Science.

Joule's achievements are remarkable. He made significant contributions to unifying the fragmented sections of physics, was the first to calculate the velocity of gas molecules, was one of the first scientists to recognize the need for standard units of electricity, showed how to calculate the heat produced by an electric current moving through a wire (now known as Joule's law) and, with Thomson, discovered that gases lose heat when they expand in a vacuum, a find that led directly to the subsequent invention of the refrigerator. Yet his greatest scientific legacy was in demonstrating the validity of the principle of energy conservation. This formed the basis of the First Law of Thermodynamics, which states that energy can neither be created nor destroyed, though it can be changed from one form to another, and has been described as 'one of the most important generalizations in the history of science'.[28] Joule made it clear that his appetite for scientific knowledge was fuelled by his faith: 'After the knowledge of, and obedience to, the will of

God, the next aim must be to know something of his attributes of wisdom, power and goodness as evidenced by his handiwork. It is evident that an acquaintance with natural laws means no less than an acquaintance with the mind of God therein expressed.'[29] Elsewhere he wrote, 'The phenomena of nature, whether mechanical, chemical, or vital, consist almost entirely in a continual conversion ... into another. Thus it is that order is maintained in the universe. Nothing is deranged, nothing ever lost, but the entire machinery, complicated as it is, works smoothly and harmoniously ... the whole being governed by the sovereign will of God.'[30]

Born in Northern Ireland, mathematical physicist *William Thomson* (1824-1907) was an astonishing achiever by any standard. He matriculated at the University of Glasgow when he was just ten years of age and two years later won a prize for translating Lucian's *Dialogues* from Latin. At seventeen, already a teenage prodigy, he moved to Cambridge, where he graduated four years later. While at Cambridge he showed a lively interest in classics, music and literature, won the single-seater Silver Sculls at rowing and was a member of the winning crew in the annual Oxford-Cambridge boat race. After studying research techniques in France he lectured briefly in Cambridge, becoming a Fellow of Peterhouse, before being elected Professor of Natural Philosophy at Glasgow University. He was just twenty-two and had already published fifty mathematical papers, mainly in French.

He combined his lecturing with active research in a laboratory he had set up in a cellar, his particular interests being heat, electricity and magnetism. He eventually established what is now known as the Kelvin Scale of absolute temperature, the name being taken from the title Baron Kelvin of Largs, which the government conferred on him in 1892. His conclusion that 'Electricity is to be understood as not an accident, but an essence of matter,' led his contemporary James Clerk Maxwell (see below) to develop the theory of electromagnetism. Thomson remained in his post for fifty-three years — then promptly enrolled as a research student, thus becoming not only one of the youngest, but also one of the oldest students in the university's history.

Thomson had a major role in developing the Second Law of Thermodynamics, the dynamic theory of heat and the rational analysis of electromagnetism, and did fundamental work in hydrodynamics. He also achieved popular fame for the design and development of the mirror-galvanometer used in the first successful sustained transmissions by means of a submarine cable laid between Ireland and Newfoundland.

Knighted in 1866, Thomson published 661 papers on scientific subjects and patented seventy inventions. Awarded twenty-one honorary doctorates, he was said to have been entitled to more letters after his name than any other man in the British Commonwealth. He joined the Royal Society in 1851, won its Royal Medal in 1856 and its Copley Medal in 1883, and was its President from 1889-1895. He also served as President of the British Association for the Advancement of Science and three times as President of the Royal Edinburgh Society.

In all of his theoretical and practical work Thomson remained a convinced and articulate Christian. He believed that the coherence of nature and Scripture could be established with 'sober, scientific certainty'[31] and saw God as 'maintaining and sustaining his creation through the exercise of his will'.[32] Although Charles Darwin branded him 'an odious spectre', his convictions remained crystal clear: 'Overwhelmingly strong proofs of intelligence and design lie around us'; 'I believe that the more thoroughly science is studied, the further does it take us from anything comparable to atheism'; 'The atheistic idea is so nonsensical that I can't put it into words.'[33]

The last in our sample of pioneering giants is the Scottish scientist *James Clerk Maxwell* (1831-1879), now generally recognized as the father of modern physics. Educated at home in his early years, he went to Edinburgh University when he was sixteen, though he later transferred to Cambridge. He was prodigiously studious and worked far into the night. It is said that when he arrived at Cambridge and was told that there would be a compulsory church service at 6 a.m., he thoughtfully stroked his beard and replied, 'Aye, I suppose I could stay up that late'! He was eventually appointed to professorships at Marischal College, Aberdeen, and Kings College London, before moving back to Cambridge as its first Cavendish Professor of Physics in 1871. Almost immediately he set about planning and designing the Cavendish Laboratory of Physics, which now has a global reputation for excellence.

Maxwell made huge contributions to classical and statistical thermodynamics, physics and mathematics. His work was significantly used in later discoveries, such as the theory of relativity and quantum theory, and it seems generally agreed that all of modern electronics is based on the mathematical equations elaborated by Maxwell. He defined the nature of gases, expressed all the fundamental laws of light, electricity and magnetism, provided the tools to create the technological age, from radio to radar and television to the mobile telephone — and took the first-ever colour photograph. Albert Einstein said that Maxwell had introduced a new scientific epoch and that his electromagnetic theory was 'the most profound and most fruitful that physics has experienced since the time of Newton'.[34] Maxwell's faith in God lay behind all his work; he once wrote, 'I have looked into most philosophical systems and I have seen not one that will work without a God.'[35] He was noted for his extemporaneous prayers, at least one of which has been preserved: 'Teach us to study the works of thy hands, that we may subdue the earth to our use and strengthen our reason for thy service.'[36]

Far from our having had to scrape the barrel to find these twelve examples, they are no more than a small sample of a much larger 'hall of fame'. Here in passing are another twelve:

- Georgias Agricola, acknowledged as the father of metallurgy.

- Johannes Baptista van Helmont, the founder of pneumatic chemistry.
- Francesco Grimaldi, who discovered the refraction of light.
- Antionie van Leeuwenhoek, who first identified bacteria.
- Neils Steno, the founder of modern geology.
- John Dalton, the founder of modern atomic theory.
- Louis Pasteur, the founder of physio-chemistry.
- Samuel Morse, the inventor of the electric telegraph.
- John Herschel, one of the greatest-ever astronomers.
- Joseph Lister, who revolutionized antiseptic surgery.
- Alexander Fleming, who discovered penicillin.
- Matthew Maury, the founder of modern oceanography.

Each one of the twenty-four men listed on these last few pages was an outstanding scientist who believed that the entire universe is the creative work of God, that the Bible is the Word of God and that there was no contradiction between his scientific knowledge and Christian convictions that had been carefully examined and could be confidently asserted. Then what do we make of Peter Atkins's claim that science is incompatible with belief in God? Is he suggesting that none of these outstanding men meets his criteria for being 'a true scientist'? The only alternative seems to be the assertion that, although their science was excellent, they mysteriously lost touch with reality as soon as they turned to religion. Nor does his statement that religion is 'armchair speculation well suited to adipose brains' find any sensible traction in these testimonies. Dictionaries define 'adipose' as 'fat', 'fatty', or 'used for the storage of fat'. As size is obviously not the issue, the only other clue we have is the phrase 'armchair speculation', which seems to hint at lazy or careless thinking. Is he really saying that these giants were lazy fatheads? Granting Atkins all the licence his words will allow, his statements seem to stem from prejudiced rhetoric rather than from principled reasoning. For Richard Dawkins to call faith 'stupefied superstition'[37] is to be equally at odds with the evidence.

Update

The last of these twenty-four giants died in the middle of the twentieth century, but the position today is essentially no different. All over the world there are outstanding scientists who are men of God as well as men of science. Two modern thinkers have gone even further: 'A significant number of scientists, historians of science and philosophers of science see more scientific evidence now for a personal creator and designer than was available fifty years ago. In the light of this evidence, it is false and naïve to claim that modern science has made belief in the supernatural unreasonable.'[38] We shall allow two outstanding scientists, in very different disciplines, to speak for all of them.

Raymond Jones is a distinguished agricultural scientist. A Fellow of the Australian Institute of Agricultural Science, the Australian Academy of Technological Science and Engineering and the Tropical Grasslands Society of Australia, he has published about 140 research papers and has been honoured with the Urrbrae Award and the CSIRO Gold Medal for Research Excellence.

Jones's fame is especially linked with his solving of an unusual and costly problem. The shrubby tree *Leucaena* is a nutritious legume that remains suitable for grazing even in the dry season, but it contains a toxin that made Australian animals sick. Jones discovered that this did not happen in places such as Hawaii and Indonesia, and suggested that perhaps this was because they had different bacteria in the rumen, a special 'stomach' where the animals' food was predigested. Other scientists scoffed at the idea, but when rumen fluid from Indonesian goats was transferred to others from Australia it took just two days to prove his theory. Eventually, microbes from goats isolated in Hawaii were shown to be new to science and named *Synergistes jonesii* in his honour. His discovery is worth millions of dollars a year to Australia and the savings are growing by the year.

In his early years Jones was a staunch evolutionist, but while at university his beliefs were shaken by the fact that he could not find evidence for the multitudes of intermediate forms which should exist if evolution were true. Asked in an interview whether evolution had great practical value, Jones replied, 'In my experience, I've never seen that. Many scientists might speculate in their papers about how a certain result relates to evolution, but I don't see that it's the driving force that enables breakthroughs, or that it features much in most scientists' work. Is having an evolutionary paradigm more enabling of research? I don't think so. In fact, believing in an almighty God, rather than chance, behind everything could be more of a driving force for your scientific work. It gives you confidence that something will be found when you search, because behind it all is a mind greater than your own.'[39]

Francis Collins trained as a physical chemist, then went to medical school and became a physician. An expert in the genetics of human disease, he was part of the team that identified the genes defective in cystic fibrosis, Huntington's disease and neurofibromatosis. He is now the director of America's National Human Genome Research Laboratory, which plays the leading role in the Human Genome Project, arguably the most important biological project of our time. He says that in his early twenties he was 'a pretty obnoxious atheist', but at twenty-seven he became a convinced and committed Christian, largely through the writings of C. S. Lewis.

In the course of an interview, Collins said, 'I think it's critical that we have a meaningful dialogue between people of faith and people involved in science, and ideally it would be nice if some of those were the same people. I see no reason why that can't be the case. In fact, as a scientist, the religious aspects of my life, I believe, add additional meaning to what I do in science.' Asked to elaborate, he replied, 'As a geneticist, I'm in the situation, particularly with the revolution that is going on in genetics, of observing new things all the time. Running the genome project, hardly a week goes by where some gene isn't discovered that plays a critical role in understanding a disease that had been completely obscure until now. That is a remark-able experience, particularly if you have the chance to be part of the actual moment of discovery, which I have had on a few occasions. For me, as a person of faith, that moment of discov-ery has an additional dimension. It's appreciating something, realizing something, knowing something that until then no human had known — but God knew it. There is an intricacy and elegance in the nature of biology, particularly when it comes to the information-carrying capacity of DNA, which is rather awesome. There is a sense in which those moments of discovery also become moments of worship, moments of appreciation, of the incredible intricacies and beauty of biology, of the world, of life — and therefore an appreciation of God as the Creator.'[40] Elsewhere, he wrote, 'Of all choices, atheism requires the greatest faith, as it demands that one's limited store of human knowledge is sufficient to exclude the possibility of God.'[41]

We leave the last word in this chapter to Colin Russell, Emeritus Professor of Science and Technology at the Open University: 'To portray Christian and scientific doctrines as persistently in conflict is not only historically inaccurate, but actually a caricature so grotesque that what needs to be ex-plained is how it could possibly have achieved any degree of respectability…'[42]

7.
Beyond science

Professor David Horrobin, who died in 2003, has been de-scribed as 'one of the most original minds of his generation'.[1] With two medical degrees and a doctorate in neuroscience, he taught medicine at Magdalen College, Oxford, and was then Professor of Medical Physiology at the University of Nairobi in Kenya before returning to the UK to become Reader in Medical Physiology at the University of Newcastle. Three years later he became Professor of Medicine at the University of Montreal. In 1979 he set up a pharmaceutical company that was to make landmark discoveries within two technologies (lipids and photo-dynamic therapy) in the fields of cancer, dermatology and diabetes. Eighteen years later, in order to concentrate on research in psychiatry, he and his wife set up another company developing pharmaceuticals for psychiatric and neurodegenera-tive disorders such as Huntington's disease, depression and schizophrenia. As the author or editor of numerous books and a contributor to more than 800 publications, we can fairly call David Horrobin a truly outstanding scientist. His appearance here stems from a book he wrote in 1969: its title was *Science is God*.

At first glance, this title seems to answer the question, 'Has Science got rid of God?', with an emphatic 'Yes' — but as the following quotations will show, Horrobin took a very different tack:

> Science is the modern god... Twentieth-century scien-
> tists ... make the wildest claims on behalf of their god ...
> and bewildered twentieth-century common men have a
> crude faith in their god which they do not care to have
> questioned too closely. [2]

> Ultimately the psychologist, the psychiatrist, the soci-
> ologist must each confess that his work must be prefaced
> by 'I believe' and not by 'I have proved scientifically'. [3]

Far from saying that science had usurped God, Horrobin was
underlining the message of the American scientist Anthony
Standen's best-seller *Science is a Sacred Cow*, published in
1950. In simple terms, he was saying that modern man has
wrongly elevated science from a discipline to a deity, whose
authority is absolute and before whom all other claims to truth
must submit.

A recap

This is where we came in. Dr Roy Peacock, Managing Director
of Thermodyne and Visiting Professor of Aerospace at the
University of Pisa, Italy, says that soon after he became a
Christian he concluded that '... the great divide between the
Christian faith and scientific knowledge is a mirage promoted by
a few noisy people.'[4] This may be the case, but the 'noisy
people' are the ones who are being heard the most. The issue
of origins provides a good example.

In his book *Testing Darwinism*, Phillip Johnson refers to the
play *Inherit the Wind*, a fictionalized treatment of the famous
1925 'Scopes Trial', in which a young teacher was accused of
violating a law prohibiting the teaching of evolution in Ten-
nessee schools. The play cleverly succeeds in making the case
for the defence look perfectly reasonable, but has the prosecut-
ing attorney making such a mess of his final speech that the

programme director switches him off and replaces the live outside broadcast with recorded music from the Chicago studio. Johnson maintains that while the play did not create a stereotype of the public debate on the issue, '... it presented it in a powerful story that sticks in the minds of journalists, scientists and intellectuals generally.'[5] He then makes the point that those with the power to turn the microphone on or off decide what the world at large will hear: 'When the creation-evolution conflict is replayed in our own media-dominated times, the microphone-owners of the media get to decide who plays the heroes and who plays the villains.'[6] As the current 'official' story is one of a universe existing and developing by an ongoing succession of mindless events, those who maintain that a transcendent God is the creator and sustainer of it all are often marginalized or ridiculed.

Science now has such a high profile (and brilliant track record) that in public debate religion is often derided or dismissed, reflecting Peter Atkins's claim that science can explain everything. This 'cool' dismissal of religion is ignited by Richard Dawkins, who calls a biblical belief system 'ignominious, contemptible and retarded'.[7] However, in chapter 2 we drew the distinction between science and *scientism* and showed that the latter is logically unsustainable, as it is only by abandoning the very rules by which it justifies its own existence that it can claim that God does not exist.

When we examined true science in chapter 3 we found that 'Science says...' is not to be equated with 'The fact is...' A scientific description of an entity or event is not the only valid one; scientific claims have often been modified or replaced; and scientists of equal merit are sometimes at loggerheads over important ideas or theories. Even more tellingly, we saw that vast areas of knowledge are beyond the reach of science, making its aims much shorter than its claims. For all its brilliant achievements, science is unable to tell us why the universe came into being, why there are consistent and dependable natural laws, why fundamental physical constants are so fine-

tuned as to support intelligent life on our planet, why we are
persons and not merely animate objects, or why the mind
functions as it does. Science is incapable of giving us an inner
quality of life, or of defining or explaining ethical principles. It is
unable to tell us anything about the purpose of life, or our
destiny after death. These are sobering shortcomings. To pick
up on just one of them, questions of meaning and value are
outside the limits of science, yet without a concept of meaning
how can science be justified? What is more, science is unable to
prove that God does not exist, firstly because he is spiritual and
not material, secondly because he is by definition beyond the
comprehension of finite minds, and thirdly because it is impossible to prove a universal negative.

In chapter 4 we concentrated on the theory of macro-
evolution, which for many people has become the weapon of
choice in attacking God. Relentlessly promoted in educational
circles and in the media, the idea has become so pervasive that
Sir Julian Huxley called it 'the most powerful and the most
comprehensive idea that has ever arisen on earth'.[8] Yet in a
single chapter we were able to show that it fell far short of being
provable. There is no solid evidence of intermediate life forms
between any of the major groupings — *homo sapiens*, apelike
quadrupeds, birds, reptiles, amphibians, vertebrate fishes,
metazoan invertebrates and microscopic single-cell organisms.
In spite of Herculean efforts to find them, the missing links are
all missing! Nor is there a shred of objective evidence to show
that life arose on our planet as the result of an accidental
collision of inert elements in some kind of chemical soup.

Leaning on the 'synthetic theory' that, given an immense
amount of time, mutations could pave the way for natural
selection to create new orders of animals has proved just as
futile, especially since the discovery of DNA, with its staggering
'cargo' of genetic information. As there is no natural law or
physical process by which information can be generated or
increased, macro-evolution is stuck at the starting-gate. As
John Baumgardner puts it, 'If ever there was in the history of

mankind clear evidence for creation, evidence for a Super-Intelligence behind what we see today, it's the genetic code. Incredibly complex information structures, coded in DNA, form the genetic blueprints for every living organism. Evolutionists have absolutely no clue as to how such structures could arise by natural processes, much less how the code itself could come into existence.'[9]

The Israeli biophysicist Dr Lee Spetner, who taught information and communication theory at Johns Hopkins University, is equally adamant: 'The neo-Darwinians would like us to believe that large evolutionary changes can result from a series of small events if there are enough of them. But if these events all lose information they can't be the steps in the kind of evolution [the neo-Darwinian theory] is supposed to explain, no matter how many mutations there are. Whoever thinks macroevolution can be made by mutations that lose information is like the merchant who lost a little money on every sale but thought he could make it up on volume.'[10]

The 'information by accident' idea disintegrates as soon as we touch it. If the information in the human genetic code is something that evolved as the result of an unimaginable amount of genetic damage, why should it mean anything to us? If our brains tell us they are merely the products of blind chemical actions and reactions, how can we know that even this message is the truth?

Chapter 5 established that true scientists are men and women of faith, necessarily committed to belief in their own existence, the objective and independent reality of the universe, the uniformity of nature, the integrity of their own senses, the law of cause and effect and the existence of invisible reality. It also showed that all of these assumptions fit perfectly into a biblical world-view, with God at its centre. Finally, it showed that far from being a vague amalgamation of religious ideas, Christianity is firmly rooted in verifiable history.

This was endorsed in chapter 6, in which we listened to some of the greatest scientists in history confirming that there was no dichotomy between their scientific knowledge and their faith in God. Today, thousands of other scientists, many of them with outstanding credentials, give the same testimony, something that came home to me very strikingly when I preached at a normal Sunday morning church service in which the congregation of 300 included over thirty scientists with earned doctorates in disciplines ranging from medicine to microbiology and from pharmacy to physics.

From nothing to nowhere?

Godless science not only has the fatal flaws we have revisited here; it also comes with some very disheartening baggage.

In 1995 Peter Atkins wrote an article which was published in the *Independent* with the title, 'A desolate place to look for answers', and the sub-title, 'The meaning of life in our universe is not as perplexing as it is depressing.' The article concluded like this: 'Where did it come from? From nothing. Where is it going? To oblivion. How is it getting there? By purposeless decay into chaos. And the cosmic purpose? I leave you to draw your own conclusions.'[11]

Bertrand Russell filled out the bleak scenario that materialism offers: 'Brief and powerless is man's life; on him and on all his race the slow, sure doom falls, pitiless and dark. Blind to good and evil, reckless of destruction, omnipotent matter rolls on its relentless way; for man, condemned today to lose his dearest, tomorrow himself to pass through the gates of darkness.'[12]

Looking back on a brilliant career, film director Robert Altman shared his conclusions with readers of the *Observer*. 'If I had never lived, if the sperm that hit the egg had missed, it would have made no difference to anything.'[13]

In *The Selfish Gene*, Richard Dawkins maintains that essentially '... we are survival machines — robot vehicles blindly programmed to preserve the selfish molecules known as genes.'[14] I have always felt that this idea must be desolating to anyone without offspring, and atheist Steve Pinker, Professor of Philosophy at the Massachusetts Institute of Technology, responds to it with hollow humour: 'Well into my procreating years I am, so far, voluntarily childless, having squandered my biological resources reading and writing, doing research, helping out friends and students, and jogging in circles, ignoring the solemn imperative to spread my genes. By Darwinian standards I am a horrible mistake, a pathetic loser... But I am happy to be that way, and if my genes don't like it, they can jump in the lake.'[15] Richard Dawkins says that the publisher of a foreign translation of *The Selfish Gene* was so shattered by its cold, bleak message that he could not sleep for three nights.[16] Atheism's creed is clear and cruel: we began as a fluke, we live as a farce and we end as fertilizer.

There is an alternative...

Good news

The idea that science has got rid of God is nineteenth-century folklore masquerading as twenty-first-century fact. The contemporary British preacher Peter Lewis is right to maintain that 'Scientific discovery invites faith and challenges unbelief, rather than the reverse.'[17] Nor is God playing hide and seek with us. In his typically quirky way, the American film producer Woody Allen complained, 'If God would only speak to me — just once. If he would only cough. If I could just see a miracle. If I could see a burning bush or the seas part. Or my Uncle Sasha pick up the check.'[18] Elsewhere he mused, 'If only God would give me some clear sign! Like making a large deposit in my name at a Swiss bank.'[19] One has to smile at Allen's wit, but on this extremely serious issue he misses the point that God *has* spoken and revealed himself to us in at least three dramatic ways.

1. God has revealed himself in creation

As we have seen, atheistic science has no explanation for the existence of the universe, whereas the Bible declares, 'The heavens declare the glory of God; the skies proclaim the work of his hands.'[20] This tells us not only that God is distinct from all creation, but that creation is a stupendous signpost to his existence. Commenting on this, Kirsten Birkett writes, 'The creation account in Genesis 1 emphasizes by its highly ordered and carefully worded literary structure that God created the world as an orderly and rational place. The world is not chaotic or haphazard. It is organized and intelligible, because it owes its existence and shape to the rational creative word of an all-wise Creator... The Bible's doctrine of creation is not only thoroughly consistent with the scientific endeavour, but provides a conceptual basis for it... The very fabric of God's creation provides a rationale for the scientific enterprise.'[21]

This reflects the Bible's own insistence that in the wonders of the natural world God has revealed 'his eternal power and divine nature'.[22] Dr Arthur Compton, a Nobel Prize winner in physics, expressed his own convictions very clearly: 'For myself, faith begins with a realization that a supreme intelligence brought the universe into being and created man. It is not difficult for me to have this faith, for it is incontrovertible that where there is a plan there is intelligence. An orderly, unfolding universe testifies to the truth of the most majestic statement ever uttered — "In the beginning God." '[23]

2. God has revealed himself in the Bible

I have examined this in detail elsewhere.[24] In spite of 2,000 years of investigation, persecution, criticism and cynicism, the Bible remains intact and unscarred. Time and again sceptics have questioned its historical accuracy, only to have further research prove them wrong; not a single one of its hundreds of prophecies has been shown to be false; it sets the highest moral standards known to man and, although written by over forty authors over a period of some 1,500 years, its amazing unity is unequalled in literature of any kind. Sir Isaac Newton was hardly exaggerating when he called it 'a rock from which all the hammers of criticism have never chipped a single fragment'. Quite simply, there is no human explanation for the Bible. In every way that we can test it, it lives up to its claim to be 'the living and enduring word of God'.[25]

The Bible not only tells us of God's existence, but also reveals many of his attributes. He is *transcendently self-existent*, 'the eternal God'[26] who is 'from everlasting to everlasting',[27] above and beyond time, space and all other reality. He is *immutable*; he 'does not change like shifting shadows',[28] and is never moulded or manipulated by circumstances or experience. He is actively *omnipotent* and 'works out everything in conformity with the purpose of his will'.[29] He is *omniscient* — 'perfect in knowledge'[30] — so that he never has to learn, discover or remember anything. He is utterly *holy*; he cannot 'look on evil'[31] and '… in him there is no darkness at all.'[32] In the words of the nineteenth-century American theologian James Boyce, God's holiness is 'the sum of all excellence and the combination of all the attributes which constitute perfection of character'.[33]

Finally, 'God is *love*.'[34] Love is of his very essence, and its depth and breadth are utterly beyond our limited human understanding. This does not mean that he is a 'soft touch', or some kind of celestial sugar-daddy, indulgently lavishing his benevolence on all and sundry in a way that is indifferent to their beliefs and behaviour. Although the Bible speaks of his 'unfailing kindness'[35] and 'wonderful love',[36] it also shows that this love is focused on his purpose to bring people into an eternal relationship with himself.

Madalyn Murray O'Hair, founder and president of American Atheists Inc., famously filed a lawsuit which in 1963 resulted in the United States Supreme Court banning organized prayer in public schools. Dubbed 'the most hated woman in America', she and two of her children disappeared (along with over

$500,000 of American Atheist funds) and six years later her burned and dismembered body was found on a remote Texas ranch. She was renowned for her bitter and crude attacks on Christianity, spoke of 'the insanity of believing in God' and said, 'There's absolutely no conclusive proof [that Jesus] ever really existed.'[37] Yet in her diary she repeatedly wrote, 'Somebody, somewhere, love me!'[38] It is a tragic irony that she made a career out of arrogantly rejecting the one whose love is so 'wide and long and high and deep' that it 'surpasses knowledge'.[39]

3. God has revealed himself in Jesus Christ

We saw in chapter 3 that 'God is spirit' and the Bible specifically says, 'No one has ever seen God.'[40] Yet it also says that Jesus Christ 'has made him known'.[41] The phrase 'made him known' is based on the Greek verb *exegéomai*, which means 'to bring out into the open'. In the person of Jesus we have an accessible revelation of the very nature and character of God. In the Bible's amazing words, 'In Christ all the fulness of the Deity lives in bodily form.'[42] He was as fully man as if he were not God, and as fully God as if he were not man. Richard Bube puts it like this: 'God has taken the attributes of his being — his love, his mercy, his holiness, his justice, his power — and has translated them into a form that men can understand, believe and respond to... The climax of God's revelation of himself is the person of Jesus Christ. In him the ultimate and the unconditional are wed to the transient and the conditioned in such a way that a human being can respond with his or her own personality.'[43]

The distinguished space scientist Sir Robert Boyd was at one time Professor of Astronomy at the Royal Institution and was also Emeritus Professor of Physics at the University of London. A Fellow of the Royal Society, he was not only a world-class scientist but also a quietly influential Christian. When he died in 2004, an obituary in the *Daily Telegraph* paid him this tribute: 'Throughout his life he was a man of strong religious faith that was entirely rational and committed; he saw no incompatibility between the honest pursuit of scientific truth and the claims of the Christian Gospel.'[44]

When he was Director of the Mullard Space Laboratory at Holmbury St Mary, in Surrey, he wrote a poem for a Christmas issue of his parish church's magazine. He says that he wrote it 'to let the village know that the head of the somewhat mysterious laboratory at the top of the hill was not at all like the "mad" scientist of tradition but a grateful and dependent disciple of Christ, as were many of his colleagues'. This shortened version[45] includes a powerful presentation of the fact that in the birth of Jesus Christ some 2,000 years ago God 'became flesh and', for a while, 'made his dwelling among us':[46]

'In the beginning', long before all worlds,
Or flaming stars or whirling galaxies,
Before that first 'big bang', if such it was,
Or earlier contraction: back and back
Beyond all time or co-related space
And all that is and all that ever was
And all that yet will be; Source of the whole,
'In the beginning was the Word' of God.

Who is this God, and can this God be known
Within the confines of a human skull,
A litre and a half of mortal brain
Whose interlinking neurons must depend
On chemistry or physics in the end,
For all that man can know or comprehend?
Can man know God eternally enthroned
Throughout all space and in the great beyond?

The mystery of being, still unsolved
By all our science and philosophy,
Fills me with breathless wonder, and the God
From whom it all continually proceeds

Calls forth my worship and shall worship have.
But love in incarnation draws my soul
To humble adoration of a Babe;
'In this was manifest the love of God.'

Still Jesus comes to those who seek for God
And still he answers as he did of old,
'I've been with you so long, how can you say,
"I don't know God, oh, show me God today!"?
When you've met me you've seen the eternal God,
Met him as Father too, as he who cares
And loves and longs for men as I myself.
I am the Christmas message. God has come.'

The Saviour

Yet the Bible makes it clear that, as well as giving us in human
flesh and form a revelation of his nature, God had another
specific reason for coming into the world in this way: 'For God
so loved the world that he gave his one and only Son, that
whoever believes in him shall not perish but have eternal life.'[47]
Elsewhere we are told that Jesus 'came into the world to save
sinners'.[48] He did not come as a statesman, a politician, a
philosopher, a financial adviser, a psychiatrist or a doctor, but in
order to save us from the appalling consequences of our inbuilt
rejection of God and his ways.

Jesus came on a rescue mission — at the cost of his own life.
The Bible says that '... all have sinned and fall short of the glory
of God,'[49] and that '... the wages of sin is death.'[50] Sin separates
us from God, not only in this life but in the life to come:
'Nothing impure will ever enter [heaven].'[51] This means that, left
to ourselves, we are guilty, lost and helpless, yet 'God demonstrates his own love for us in this: While we were still sinners,
Christ died for us.'[52] In his dreadful death by crucifixion the
sinless Jesus took the place of sinners, becoming as accountable

for their sins as if he had been responsible for them. God is unutterably holy and cannot leave any sin unpunished, so that when Jesus took the place of sinners he had to bear in full the penalty their sins deserved. On the cross Jesus was exposed to the full extent of God's wrath against the sinners he represented and the sins they had committed.

The only completely innocent person in all of human history voluntarily took upon himself the physical and spiritual death penalty that sin deserves and God demands. Nothing was held back, and in bearing the penalty for the sins of others Jesus had such an appalling sense of separation from his Father that he cried out, 'My God, my God, why have you forsaken me?'[53] We may never be able to know all that this meant; we are faced with 'a mystery which no painting or sculpture, with distorted face, can ever show'.[54] What we *do* know is that in the death of his Son, God 'demonstrates his own love for us'. One of the early Christians wrote of 'the Son of God, who loved me and gave himself for me';[55] another stated, 'For Christ died for sins once for all, the righteous for the unrighteous, to bring you to God;[56] while yet another added, 'This is how we know what love is: Jesus Christ laid down his life for us.'[57]

But the most gruesome day in human history was followed soon afterwards by the most glorious, when the resurrection of Jesus from the dead infallibly confirmed that his sacrifice had accomplished its intention. As we saw in chapter 5, accepting that Jesus rose from the dead is not a leap in the dark. It is based on an immovable mass of incontrovertible evidence, what the Bible calls 'many convincing proofs'.[58] This is the very heart of the Christian gospel; it is the best news anyone has ever heard.

Believing and believing

When speaking to audiences about the nature of Christian faith I have often made use of the following formula. Dealing specifically with what Christian faith involves, I have said something like this: 'I believe in a cold bath before breakfast every morning. I don't just mean in the height of summer, but all the year round, even when the temperature is below zero and icicles are hanging from the guttering. I believe there is no better way to start the day than by getting smartly out of bed, running a cold bath and jumping straight in.' This has always produced a corporate wince from the audience — followed by a sudden burst of laughter as soon as I have added, 'But I have never had one!'

We have reached that point in this book, and to press the point home I am going to write these final few pages in the second personal singular. Nowhere have I tried to *prove* that God exists, because proving such a thing deductively is impossible. Instead, I have tried to show that the evidence, including the most recent scientific discoveries, *points in that direction*, and that millions of people over thousands of years (including countless scientists with outstanding credentials) have become convinced that this is the case. As you come towards the end of the book, you may have joined them. You may have read the first page as an atheist, an agnostic, or a sceptic of some kind. Now you have come to see the force of the accumulated evidence and to accept that '… there is but one God, the Father, from whom all things came…'[59]

So far, so good — but this falls a long way short of the faith the Bible requires of us. To believe in God can obviously not mean *less* than giving intellectual assent to propositional truth; the Bible makes the obvious point that '… anyone who comes to him must believe that he exists.'[60] But another New Testament writer makes it equally clear that acknowledging God's existence is not enough: 'You believe that there is one God. Good! Even the demons believe that — and shudder.'[61] The Bible gives us clear examples of this. When two demon-possessed men met Jesus, they cried out, 'What do you want with us, Son of God?'[62] On another occasion an evil spirit possessing a man shouted, 'What do you want with us, Jesus of Nazareth? Have you come to destroy us? I know who you are

— the Holy One of God!'[63] These outbursts dramatically underline the point. Faith that consists merely of giving mental assent to certain facts leaves the person concerned knowing the truth but not changed by it. In direct contrast, biblical faith enables a Christian to say, 'Therefore, since we have been justified through faith, *we have peace with God* through our Lord Jesus Christ.'[64]

The key to understanding the difference between 'head faith' and 'heart faith' is to realize that 'heart faith' means responding to a living person, not to a logical proposition. C. S. Lewis put his finger on the spot: 'To believe that God — at least *this* God — exists is to believe that you as a person now stand in the presence of God as a Person… You are no longer faced with an argument which demands your assent, but with a Person who demands your confidence.'[65]

There is a sense in which God is beyond our knowing — and we can certainly never know him purely through our own powers of reasoning. God is not part of his creation and he is not known in the way we know things he has made. Biblical belief in God is vitally different from belief in a scientific hypothesis. Even if we stack up all the evidence pointing to God's existence, we are a long way from experiencing a personal relationship with him, just as we can know a great deal *about* other people without actually *knowing* them. Colin Humphreys, Professor of Materials Science at Cambridge University, puts it like this: 'Scientific truth is mainly objective (e.g. the pen I am writing this with has a certain mass which can be measured and agreed upon by scientists throughout the world). Christian truth is both objective and subjective, and the subjective part is important. Many aspects of reality can be known only by personal involvement, for example the love of one person for another. The Christian truth that God committed himself to us through Jesus can only be known if we commit ourselves to him.'[66]

We can take this further and say that demanding evidence before believing in God (in the style of Woody Allen) is to be condemned, not commended. It is a sign of human arrogance, compounded by the fact that part of us *wants* science to be in conflict with God. Kirsten Birkett pinpoints this particular problem: 'We would all prefer to dispense with God, if that were possible. We *want* science's answers to be good enough to contend with God's answers, or render them obsolete... To have to trust that God is the only one who gives the ultimate answers is rather belittling. It does not sit well with our pride as human beings.'[67] Our fallen spiritual nature includes an inbuilt moral resistance to God, a refusal to admit our need for him, yet without admitting that need we shall remain 'without hope and without God in the world'.[68]

The Bible says that God's revelation of himself in creation alone is sufficient to leave us 'without excuse'[69] if we deny his existence. Strictly speaking, nobody is an atheist. All rational human beings have programmed into their constitutions an inner awareness of deity, a knowledge at some level of their thinking that God exists. The eighteenth-century German physicist G. C. Lichtenberg went so far as to say, 'Belief in God is an instinct as natural to man as walking on two legs,'[70] while even the French existentialist Jean-Paul Sartre admitted, 'Everything in me calls for God.'[71] The Canadian novelist Douglas Coupland became world-famous through his book *Generation X: Tales of an Accelerated Culture*, published in 1991, in which he identified with those who were born in the 1960s and 1970s and who had abandoned commitment, idealism and religion. But in a later book, *Life After God*, he wrote, 'My secret is that I need God — that I am sick and can no longer make it alone.'[72] All of us share Coupland's 'secret', yet by nature we suppress this instinct, distort its message — and fatally deceive ourselves. As a result, there is a sense in which at one and the same time we both know God and do not know him. True, biblical faith is the solution to this dilemma.

The turning point

In biblical terms, believing in God involves *turning* and *trusting* — and the second aspect is impossible without the first. The Bible's word for *turning* is 'repentance', which calls for a revolution in heart, mind and will — and God 'commands all people everywhere to repent'.[73] It means ending your rebellion against God and abandoning your self-centred independence. It means acknowledging that God has the prior claim on your life and recognizing that your primary goal should be to bring glory to him through your wholehearted obedience. It means setting your heart on living the kind of life that reflects his purity, love and grace.

As we have already seen, when the Bible speaks of believing it means something far more than the cold acceptance of facts. It means *trusting*. God promises the forgiveness of sins, eternal life and his own presence and power to enable you to live a God-centred life — but there must first be a wholehearted response to Jesus Christ. He is 'able to save completely those who come to God through him'[74] — *but you must come*, acknowledging your need of a Saviour from the power and penalty of your sin and casting yourself upon him, trusting him to do for you something that is beyond the reach not only of science, but of sincerity, respectability or religion. A world-class scientist gives us just the right picture. Writing about the nature of faith in a personal God, the German physicist Werner Heisenberg, who was awarded the 1927 Nobel Prize for Physics, stated, 'If I have faith, it means that I have decided to do something and I am willing to stake my life on it.'[75]

This is exactly what becoming a true Christian involves — abandoning all trust in your own knowledge, merits and achievements and staking your destiny on Jesus Christ, trusting him as your Saviour and submitting to him as your Lord. To do this is not to reject or abandon reason or scientific principles, but to go beyond both and to join millions of others who, over thousands of years, have found God to be true to his word, and whose search for greater truth than science could ever uncover has led them to a life-transforming relationship with their Creator. The Bible's promise could not be clearer:

> ... if you look for [wisdom] as silver
>   and search for it as for hidden treasure,
> then you will understand the fear of the LORD
>   and find the knowledge of God.[76]

Appendix
The strange story of Christian Science

Christian Science (or the Church of Christ Scientist, to give it its full name) is a rather 'quiet' organization, rarely hitting the headlines and recognized by most people only by its rather austere-looking Reading Rooms. Although never having a vast membership, it has a quite distinctive profile and is worth taking a look at, not least because of its name's apparent claim to link science and Christianity.

Phineas Parkhurst Quimby (1802-1866) lived in the north-eastern United States, and has been variously described as a master clockmaker and inventor and 'an ignorant, nonreligious blacksmith'.[1] In his early thirties he became fascinated by hypnosis and soon became an expert mesmerist, developing a philosophy he referred to by various names, including 'Science of Life and Happiness'. His medicine-free healing techniques were based on the theory that disease was due to false reasoning and that truth was the cure for all illness. He soon established a growing reputation as a healer, but he would probably warrant no more than a footnote in history had he not been consulted in 1862 by one particular patient.

Mary Ann Morse Baker, born in Bow, New Hampshire, in 1821, was the sixth and youngest child of God-fearing farming parents. Highly sensitive, intensely religious and a devout Bible student, she was chronically sick from childhood onwards, her problems including paralysis, hysteria, seizures and convulsions. By her early forties, and having dabbled in hypnosis, autosuggestion and clairvoyance, she went to Portland, Maine, to consult Phineas Quimby.

Quimby convinced her that illness and disease could be cured through positive thoughts and healthy attitudes (in other words, by changing one's beliefs about the very nature of sickness). Although some of her own symptoms were to return, she not only insisted that Quimby had fundamentally healed her, but developed a psychic dependence on him, even claiming visitations by his apparition.[2]

A few weeks after Quimby's death Mary Patterson (as she was by then) suffered a life-threatening fall on a frozen pavement. Crippled and in severe pain, she turned to the Bible for comfort and a few days later was profoundly affected by reading the account of Jesus' healing of a paralytic man.[3] Although medical testimony denies it, the 'official' version of events says that she found herself being miraculously healed.[4] She immediately set about pulling together her interpretation of the Bible's teaching with that of Phineas Quimby, and was later to claim, 'In the year 1866 I discovered the Christ Science or divine laws of Life, Truth and Love, *and named my discovery Christian Science.*'[5]

She began conducting healing sessions and teaching her healing techniques and spiritual philosophy to interested students (at an exorbitant $300 for a course of twelve lessons). She also began writing on the subject and in 1875 produced her blockbuster *Science and Health with Key to the Scriptures.* While referring to 'manifest mistakes' in the Bible, she made no bones about the origin and integrity of her own work, which she said was 'echoing the harmonies of heaven in divine metaphysics'. Not surprisingly, she claimed, 'I cannot be super-modest in my estimate of the Christian Science method.'[6] Not everybody agreed. Her literary adviser, James Henry Wiggins, was appalled at what he found: 'The misspelling, capitalization and punctuation were dreadful, but these were not the things that fazed me... There were passages that flatly and absolutely contradicted things that had preceded, and scattered all through

were incorrect references to historical and philosophical matters.' He decided that the only way to tackle his task was 'to
begin absolutely at the first page and rewrite the whole thing'[7]
— a fairly devastating indictment of a book said to have been
dictated by God!

By this time Mary Baker's first husband, George Glover, had
died, she had divorced her second, Daniel Patterson, on the
grounds of desertion (he left her because of her 'fits') and had
married Asa Gilbert Eddy (giving her age as forty, although she
was by then fifty-six). She was now entitled to call herself Mary
Ann Morse Baker Glover Patterson Eddy, but chose to be
known simply as Mary Baker Eddy when in 1879 she founded
the first Christian Science church, in Boston, Massachusetts
(renamed the First Church of Christ Scientist thirteen years
later). In 1881 she opened the Massachusetts Metaphysical
College in Boston (it was closed and reopened in 1889) and in
1883 she became the founder and first editor of the monthly
magazine *The Christian Science Journal*. She established a
publishing company in 1898, and in 1908, two years before her
death, she founded the widely respected daily newspaper *The
Christian Science Monitor*, which has won the prestigious
Pulitzer Prize six times.

Although she believed and taught that suffering and death
were illusions of the mind, she was constantly dogged by ill-
health, repeatedly needed morphine injections and wore glasses
and dentures. She eventually died in 1910, leaving an estate
worth $3,000,000. In 1995 she was posthumously inducted
into the National Women's Hall of Fame as the only American
woman to found a worldwide religion, which at its peak in the
1930s had a membership of some 300,000.

Christian Science is not an aggressive, proselytizing church,
and its public profile is usually limited to its Reading Rooms.
The name given to these meeting places is significant, as the
church has no preachers or sermons. Instead, without giving
any explanation or interpretation, First and Second Readers are

obliged to read passages from the Bible and *Science and Health.*

The all-important question to ask here is whether the Bible and Christian Science are compatible. The simplest way to find out is to compare their teaching on major issues. Here are nine examples.

• *The authority of Scripture.* The Bible claims to be 'the living and enduring word of God'.[8] Christian Science says it has thousands of errors and that *Science and Health* is the 'first book' that has been 'unadulterated by human hypotheses'.[9]

• *The nature of God.* The Bible says that God is living and personal, the creator and ruler of all reality outside of himself: 'The LORD has established his throne in heaven, and his kingdom rules over all.'[10] Christian Science says that God is 'a divine, infinite principle'[11] and promotes the pantheistic idea that 'God is All-in-all'[12] and 'identical with nature'.[13]

• *God as a tri-unity.* The Bible teaches that God exists as three persons, the Father,[14] the Son[15] and the Holy Spirit.[16] Christian Science says, 'The theory of three persons in one God [that is, a personal Trinity or Tri-unity] suggests polytheism,'[17] and redefines the Trinity as life, truth and love.

• *The deity of Jesus Christ.* The Bible teaches that Jesus is 'the true God'.[18] Christian Science says that the words 'Jesus' and 'Christ' do not refer to the same person, that Jesus was only human and that Christ is 'the divine idea'.[19]

• *The deity of the Holy Spirit.* The Bible clearly identifies the Holy Spirit as being divine.[20] Christian Science defines him as merely 'the Science of Christianity'.[21]

• *The material world.* The Bible teaches that while 'God is Spirit',[22] he created the material universe and everything

in it.[23] Christian Science says that there is no reality except
Mind and Spirit and that '… matter is … unreal.'[24]

• *Evil, sickness and death.* The Bible teaches that sin
and sickness are everyday realities[25] and that as a result of
sin '… man is destined to die.'[26] Christian Science says,
'Man is incapable of sin, sickness and death,'[27] that all
three are 'states of mind — illusions',[28] and that '… the
only reality of sin, sickness and death is the awful fact that
unrealities seem real to human, erring belief.'[29] In practice, this means that Christian Science does not promote
'faith healing' but rather the idea that one is not really sick
at all.

• *The death and resurrection of Jesus.* The Bible says
that Jesus died on the cross to pay the penalty for human
sin, rose from the dead three days later and is eternally
alive.[30] Christian Science says, 'In Science, Christ never
died,'[31] and that he left the grave knowing that this was the
case.

• *Heaven and hell.* The Bible teaches the existence of
both heaven[32] and hell.[33] Christian Science calls heaven 'a
state of mind'[34] and hell 'mortal belief, self-imposed
agony,'[35] the result of the guilt of imagined sin.

Many other examples could be given, and all of them fleshed
out to show that by insisting that *Science and Health* was the
only way in which it could be properly understood, Mary Baker
Eddy denied the Bible's authority and integrity. An American
breakfast cereal is marketed under the name of 'Grape Nuts',
even though it contains neither grapes nor nuts. Christian
Science has an equally curious name; it is neither Christian nor
scientific.

Notes

Preface
1. Edgar Andrews, *God, Science and Evolution*, Evangelical Press, p.i.

Chapter 1 — Fine-tuning the question
1. Cited by N. McCulloch, *Barriers to Belief*, Darton, Longman & Todd, p.82.
2. J. P. Moreland, *Scaling the Secular City*, Baker Book House, pp.199-200.
3. *Oxford Dictionary of English*, 2nd edition, Oxford University Press, 2003, p.1580.
4. *Soul of Britain*, BBC2, 11 June 2000.
5. Cited by Walter R. Hearn, *Being a Christian in Science*, InterVarsity Press, p.47 (emphasis added).
6. *Oxford Dictionary of English*, p.1487.
7. John Houghton, *The Search for God*, Lion Publishing, p.143.
8. John B. Noss, *Man's Religions*, Macmillan Co., p.88.
9 See Patrick Johnstone, *Operation World*, STL Books/WEC Publications, p.216.
10. Noss, *Man's Religions*, p.88.
11. Josh McDowell and Don Stewart, *Concise Guide to Today's Religions*, Scripture Press, p.375.
12. 1 Peter 1:23.
13. Hebrews 11:3.
14. Psalm 90:2.
15. See, e.g., Matthew 28:19.
16. See Psalm 18:30.
17. See Malachi 3:6.
18. Psalm 103:8.
19. Psalm 103.19.
20. Ephesians 1:11.
21. Acts 17:31.
22. See Romans 1:1-4.
23. 1 John 5:20.
24. See John 5:24.

25. Bertrand Russell, *Why I am not a Christian,* Watts & Co., p.9.
26. *Daily Telegraph,* 28 May 1996.
27. Stephen Gaukroger, *It Makes Sense,* Scripture Union, p.33.
28. Joe Boot, *Searching for Truth,* Crossway Books, p.118 (emphasis added).
29. 2 Timothy 3:16.

Chapter 2 — Scientism: the godless god

1. Houghton, *The Search for God,* pp.13-14 (I have changed the order in which Houghton lists these four attitudes).
2. *Independent,* 15 March 2002.
3. Cited by John Currid, *Building a Christian Worldview,* ed. W. Andrew Hoffecker, Presbyterian & Reformed Publishing Company, vol. 1, p.151.
4. Donald M. MacKay, *The Clockwork Image: A Christian Perspective on Science,* Inter-Varsity Fellowship, pp.15-16.
5. Carl Sagan, 'The Shores of the Cosmic Ocean', *Cosmos,* Ballantine Books, p.4.
6. Phillip Johnson, *Reason in the Balance,* InterVarsity Press, pp.7-8.
7. Kirsten Birkett, *Unnatural Enemies,* St Matthias Press, p.38.
8. David Tyler, *Evangelical Times,* February 2001.
9. Johnson, *Reason in the Balance,* p.8.
10. See Stephen M. Barr, 'Retelling the Story of Science', in *First Things* 131 (March 2003), pp.16-25.
11. *Times Higher Educational Supplement,* 18 October 2001 (emphasis added).
12. *Independent,* 1 July 1989.
13. *Omni,* 12 (4), January 1990, pp.60-61.
14. Cited in the *Daily Telegraph,* 20 March 2003.
15. *Heart of the Matter,* BBC 1, 29 September 1996.
16. Cited in the *Daily Telegraph,* 20 March 2003.
17. *Daily Telegraph,* 20 March 2003.
18. See Barr, *First Things,* pp.16-25.
19. Richard Lewontin, 'Billions and billions of demons', in *The New York Review,* 9 January 1997, p.31 (emphasis added).
20. Richard Dawkins, *A Devil's Chaplain: Reflections on Hope, Lies, Science and Love,* Houghton Mifflin Company, p.37.
21. Birkett, *Unnatural Enemies,* p.40.
22. See Barr, *First Things,* pp.1-25 (emphasis added).
23. This section has been adapted from John Blanchard, *'Does God Believe in Atheists?',* Evangelical Press, pp.149-51.
24. David Cook, *Blind Alley Beliefs,* Pickering & Inglis, p.35.
25. *Daily Telegraph,* 13 April 1996.
26. Peter Medawar, *Advice to a Young Scientist,* Harper and Row, p.31.
27. Donald MacKay, *Where Science and Faith Meet,* Inter-Varsity Fellowship, pp.15-16.

28. Peter Atkins, *The Creation*, W. H. Freeman & Co., pp.36-7.

29. *Daily Telegraph*, 31 August 1992.

30. *Sunday Telegraph*, 1 July 1997.

31. Rodney D. Holder, *Nothing but Atoms and Molecules?*, Monarch Publications, p.21.

32. Cited by Holder, *Nothing but Atoms and Molecules?*, pp.133-4.

33. See Karl Popper, *Objective Knowledge: An Evolutionary Approach*, Oxford University Press, pp.223-4.

34. Peter Atkins, *Creation Revisited*, Penguin, p.23.

35. Martin Robinson, *The Faith of the Unbeliever*, Monarch Books, p.78.

36. Moreland, *Scaling the Secular City*, p.197.

37. Bryan Appleyard, *Understanding the Present*, Picador, p.2.

38. John 18:37.

Chapter 3 — Reality check: science and its limits

1. Cited by Robert G. Clouse, 'Francis Bacon', in *New International Dictionary of the Christian Church*, ed. J. D. Douglas, Paternoster Press, p.95.

2. Appleyard, *Understanding the Present*, pp.3-4.

3. Julian Huxley, *Uniqueness of Man*, p.280.

4. *Ibid.*, p.282.

5. Malcolm A. Jeeves and R. J. Berry, *Science, Life and Christian Belief*, Baker Books, p.49.

6. Edmund Leach, *The Listener*, 16 November 1967.

7. Adapted from Gaukroger, *It Makes Sense*, p.67.

8. *Daily Telegraph*, 12 October 1993.

9. *Sunday Times*, 10 February 2002.

10. Carl Sagan, 'Velikovsky's Challenge to Science', cassette tape 186-74, produced by the American Association for the Advancement of Science.

11. *Daily Telegraph*, 13 September 1995.

12. Karl Popper, *The Logic of Scientific Discovery*, Unwin Hyman Ltd., p.278 (emphasis added).

13. Cited by Werner Gitt, *Did God use Evolution?*, Christliche, p.10 (emphasis added).

14. Del Ratzsch, *Science and its Limits*, InterVarsity Press, p.59.

15. *Sunday Telegraph*, 28 February 1999.

16. Cited by Michael Poole, *A Guide to Science and Belief*, Lion Publishing, p.32.

17. *Soul of Britain*, BBC2, 11 June 1999.

18. *Daily Telegraph Science Extra*, 11 September 1999.

19. *Daily Telegraph*, 13 September 1995.

20. *Ibid.*

21. Edward Tryon, cited in *Science Digest*, June 1984, p.101.

22. Andrews, *God, Science and Evolution*, p.35 (emphasis added).

23. Atkins, *Creation Revisited*, p.143.

24. David Darling, *New Scientist* (2047), p.49.
25. Poole, *A Guide to Science and Belief,* p.72.
26. Stephen Hawking, *Black Holes and Baby Universes,* Bantam Books, p.90.
27. Keith Ward, *God, Chance and Necessity,* Oneworld Publications, pp.108-9.
28. Andrews, *God, Science and Evolution,* p.36.
29. Cited by Ward, *God, Chance and Necessity,* p.34.
30. J. L .Mackie, *The Miracle of Theism,* Clarendon Press, p.141.
31. See George Smoot and Keay Davidson, *Wrinkles in Time,* Avon Books, pp.110-12, 293.
32. *Ibid.,* p.110.
33. Stephen Hawking, *A Brief History of Time,* Bantam Books, p.134 (emphasis added).
34. Cited by John Polkinghorne, *One World,* SPCK, p.58.
35. John Blanchard, *Does God Believe in Atheists?,* Evangelical Press, pp.241-81.
36. John Gribbin and Martin Rees, *Cosmic Coincidences,* Bantam Books, p.247.
37. Cited by David Wilkinson, *God, the Big Bang and Stephen Hawking,* Monarch Publications, p.108.
38. Hawking, *A Brief History of Time,* p.140 (emphasis added).
39. *Sunday Telegraph,* 18 February 2001.
40. *Ibid.* (emphasis added).
41. Cited by Russell Stannard, *Doing Away with God,* Marshall Pickering, p.80.
42. Richard Dawkins, *The Selfish Gene,* Oxford University Press, p.xi.
43. Fred Hoyle, *The Nature of the Universe,* Penguin Books, pp.120-21.
44. Address to the Canadian Senate, published in *New York Review of Books,* 10 June 1999.
45. Michael Ruse, *Darwinism Defended,* Addison Wesley, p.108.
46. Francis Schaeffer, *The God who is There,* Hodder & Stoughton, p.88.
47. Atkins, *The Creation,* pp.36-7.
48. E. Squires, *Conscious Mind in the Physical World,* Adam Hilger, p.24.
49. See Barr, *First Things,* pp.16-25.
50. J. B. S. Haldane, *Possible World,* Chatto and Windus, p.209.
51. *Sunday Times Magazine,* 11 February1996.
52. *Sunday Telegraph,* 17 April 1996 (emphasis added).
53. See Barr, *First Things,* pp.16-25 (emphasis added).
54. Houghton, *The Search for God,* pp.213-14 (emphasis added).
55. Publilius Syrus, *Moral Sayings,* trans. Darius Lyman, cited in *The International Thesaurus of Quotations,* George Allen & Unwin, p.105.
56. *Daily Telegraph,* 31 August 1992.
57. Michael Ruse and Edward Wilson, 'Evolution and Ethics', in *New Scientist* 208, 17 October 1985, pp.51-2.

58. William Provine, 'Scientists, Face it! Science and Religion are Incompatible', *The Scientist*, 5 September 1988, p.10.

59. Cited in Jeeves and Berry, *Science, Life and Christian Belief*, p.230.

60. *Ibid.*, p.116.

61. *Soul of Britain*, BBC2, 11 June 2000.

62. J. S. Jones, *The Language of the Genes*, HarperCollins, p.xi.

63. John Eccles, 'Science Can't Provide Ultimate Answers', *US News & World Report*, February 1985.

64. Paul Tournier, *The Whole Person in a Broken World*, Harper & Row, p.149.

65. Ludwig Wittgenstein, *Tractatus Logico-Philosophicus*, Routledge & Kegan Paul, p.187.

66. Erwin Schrödinger, *Nature and the Greeks*, cited by David Wilkinson and David Frost, *Thinking Clearly about God and Science*, Monarch Publications, p.67.

67. Mortimer J. Adler, *The Great Ideas: A Symposium of Great Books of the Western World*, vol.1, Encyclopaedia Britannica, p.543.

68. Andrew Miller, *Real Science, Real Faith*, ed. R. J. Berry, Monarch Publications, pp.94-5.

69. John 4:24.

70. *Independent*, 15 March 2002.

71. Isaiah 55:8-9.

72. Poole, *A Guide to Science and Belief*, p.28 (emphasis added).

73. *Free Inquiry Magazine*, vol. 18.

Chapter 4 — Evolution: proof or prejudice?

1. *Great Britons*, BBC2, 25 October 2002.

2. *Daily Telegraph*, 12 February 2002.

3. Cited by M. Bowden, *The Rise of the Evolution Fraud*, Sovereign Publications, p.56.

4. Cited by H. Enoch, *Evolution or Creation?*, Evangelical Press, p.145.

5. Michael Denton, *Evolution: A Theory in Crisis*, Adler &Adler, p.70.

6. 'Iconoclast of the Century': Charles Darwin (1809-1882),' *TIME* Magazine, 31 December 1999.

7. Cited by John Wright, *Designer Universe*, Monarch Publications, p.61.

8. James Moore, *Darwin: The Life of a Tormented Evolutionist*, Warner, p.xxi.

9. H. S. Lipton, 'A Physicist looks at Evolution', *Physics Bulletin*, vol. 31 (1980), p.136.

10. Ian Taylor, *In the Minds of Men*, TFE Publishing, p.177.

11. Cited by Currid, *Building a Christian Worldview*, vol. 1, p.154 (emphasis added).

12. *Ibid.* (emphasis added).

13. H. J. Muller, 'Is Biological Evolution a Principle of Nature that has been well established by Science?' (Privately duplicated and distributed by author, 2 May 1996).

14. Ernst Mayr, *Omni* magazine, February 1983, p.74.

15. Cited by Phillip E. Johnson, *Darwin on Trial,* Monarch Publications, p.9.

16. See David L. Hull, *Darwin and his Critics: The Reception of Darwin's Theory of Evolution by the Scientific Community,* Harvard University Press, pp.155-70.

17. Cited by Don Batten, *In Six Days,* ed. John F. Ashton, Master Books, p.354.

18. Denton, *Evolution: A Theory in Crisis,* p.66.

19. Richard Dawkins, *The Blind Watchmaker,* W. W. Norton, pp.6-7.

20. *TIME* Magazine, 31 December 1999.

21. *Ape Man: The Story of Human Evolution,* Arts and Entertainment Network, 4 September 1994.

22. See Henry M. Morris and Gary E. Parker, *What is Christian Science?,* Master Books, pp.52-61.

23. Cited in *New Scientist* 160 (2154): 23.

24. See Taylor, *In the Minds of Men,* p.215.

25. Marvin Lubenow, *Bones of Contention,* Baker Books, p.65.

26. Joe White and Nicholas Comninellis, *Darwin's Demise,* Master Books, p.115.

27. Taylor, *In the Minds of Men,* p.227.

28. Bolton Davidheiser, *Evolution and the Christian Faith,* Presbyterian & Reformed Publishing Co., p.326.

29. 'Lucy — Evolution's Solitary for an Ape/Man: Her Position is Slipping Away', *Creation Research Society Quarterly,* vol. 22, No. 3 (December 1985), pp.144-5.

30. Donald Johanson and T. D. White, *Science* 203:321 (1979) 207:1104 (1980).

31. D. V. Ager, 'The Nature of the Fossil Record', *Proceedings of the Geological Association,* vol. 87, No. 2 (1976), pp.132-3.

32. David Pilbeam, 'Book Review of Leakey's Origins', *American Scientist,* vol. 66 (1978), pp.378-9.

33. David Pilbeam, 'Rearranging our Family Tree', *Human Nature* (June 1978), p.44.

34. Lubenow, *Bones of Contention,* p.7 (emphasis added).

35. *Ibid.,* p.19.

36. See Johnson, *Darwin on Trial,* p.175.

37. W. R. Bird, *The Origin of Species Revisited: The Theories of Evolution and Abrupt Appearance,* Philosophical Library, vol. 1, p.228.

38. Pilbeam, *Human Nature,* p.45.

39. Lord Zuckerman, *Beyond the Ivory Tower,* Taplinger Publishing Co., p.64.

40. Charles Darwin, *The Origin of Species,* J. M. Dent & Sons Ltd, pp.292-3.

41. David M. Raup, 'Conflicts between Darwin and Palaeontology', *Field Museum of Natural History Bulletin*, vol. 50, p.25 (emphasis added).

42. Stephen J. Gould, *The Panda's Thumb*, W. W. Norton & Co., p.104.

43. Cited by Johnson, *Darwin on Trial*, p.59 (emphasis added).

44. Cited in *The Life and Letters of Charles Darwin*, ed. Francis Darwin, vol. 1, University Press of the Pacific, p.210.

45. Sylvia Baker, *Bone of Contention*, Evangelical Press, p.19.

46. See Gary E. Parker, *Creation — The Facts of Life*, Creation-Life Publishers, p.63.

47. Julian Huxley, *Evolution in Action*, Harper & Brothers, p.41.

48. Magnus Verbrugge, *Alive: An Enquiry into the Origin and Meaning of Life*, Ross House Books, p.12.

49. Johnson, *Darwin on Trial*, p.37.

50. René Chauvin, *La biologie de l'esprit*, Editions du Rocher, pp.23-4 (emphasis added).

51. Cited by D. T. Tosevear, *Scientists Critical of Evolution*, Evolution Protest Movement, Pamphlet No. 224, July 1980, p.4.

52. Cited by E. Shute, *Flaws in the Theory of Evolution*, Craig Press, pp.127-8.

53. Cited by Parker, *Creation — The Facts of Life*, p.163.

54. Charles Darwin, *Origin of Species*, 6th edition, New York University Press, p.154 (emphasis added).

55. Leon E. Long, *Geology*, McGraw-Hill Book Company, p.172.

56. Michael Behe, Interview, 'The Evolution of a Sceptic', 10 January 1997.

57. Michael Behe, *Darwin's Black Box*, The Free Press, p.96

58. Cited by Johnson, *Darwin on Trial*, p.54.

59. Johnson, *Darwin on Trial*, p.54.

60. Wolfgang Smith, *Teilhardism and the New Religion*, Tan Books, p.2.

61. *Ibid.*, p.5.

62. Marcel P. Schutzenburger, 'Algorithims and the Neo-Darwinian Theory of Evolution', in *Mathematical Challenges to the Neo-Darwinian Interpretation of Evolution*, p.75.

63. See *Science*, vol. 210, pp.883-7.

64. R. E. D. Clark, *The Christian Stake in Science*, Paternoster Press, pp.24-5.

65. Cited by Johnson, *Darwin on Trial*, p.41.

66. Fred Hoyle, *The Intelligent Universe*, Michael Joseph, pp.20-21,23.

67. Denton, *Evolution: A Theory in Crisis*, pp.249-50.

68. *Ibid.*

69. Cited by Clark, *The Christian Stake in Science*, p.59.

70. *News Chronicle*, 17 October 1950.

71. Klaus Dose, 'The Origin of Life: More Questions than Answers', *Interdisciplinary Science Review 13* (1988), p.348.

72. George Wald, 'The Origin of Life' in *The Physics and Chemistry of Life*, Simon and Schuster, p.12.

73. F. B. Salisbury, 'Natural Selection and the Complexity of the Gene', in *Nature,* vol. 224 (217) 1969.

74. George C. Williams, cited by Phillip Johnson, *Testing Darwinism,* InterVarsity Press, p.70.

75. Johnson, *Testing Darwinism,* p.72.

76. See John Gribbin, *Creation,* Oxford University Press, pp.191-2.

77. Werner Gitt, *In the Beginning was Information,* Christliche Literatur, p.79.

78. Stephen Grocott, *In Six Days,* ed. Ashton, p.136.

79. Arthur E. Wilder-Smith in Willem J. J. Glashower and Paul S. Taylor, *The Origin of the Universe,* Eden Communications and Standard Media (emphasis added).

80. Paul Davies, *Superforce — The Search for a GUT of Nature,* Unwin Paperbacks, p.5.

81. Isaac Newton, *Principia,* cited in Donald B. De Young, *Astronomy and the Bible,* Baker Book House, p.115.

82. Private letter to the author, 25 February 1999.

83. Genesis 1:1.

84. C. S. Lewis, *Miracles,* Macmillan, p.33.

Chapter 5 — Faith and facts

1. Richard Dawkins, *New Humanist Journal,* 1996, Rationalist Press Association.

2. *Science Christian Monitor,* 4 January 1962 (emphasis added).

3. Marjorie Grene, *Encounter,* November 1959, p.49 (emphasis added).

4. Del Ratzsch, *Science & Its Limits,* InterVarsity Press, p.137.

5. Cited by Victor F. Weiskopf, 'The Frontier and Limits of Science', *American Science* 67, July-August 1977, p.405.

6. Cited by Russell Stannard, *Science and Wonders,* Faber & Faber, pp.178-9.

7. Jeeves and Berry, *Science, Life and Christian Belief,* p.97.

8. Stanley D. Beck, 'Natural Science and Creationist Theology', *Bioscience* 32, October 1982, p.739.

9. Ratzsch, *Science & Its Limits,* p.15.

10. Acts 14:15.

11. *Soul of Britain,* BBC2, 11 June 2000.

12. Ratzsch, *Science & Its Limits,* p.137.

13. Psalm 145:3.

14. Romans 11:33.

15. Cited by Wilkinson and Frost, *Thinking Clearly about God and Science,* p.33.

16. Cited by Polkinghorne, *One World,* p.63.

17. Cited by David Lindley at www.douglashospital.qc.ca

18. See Barr, *First Things,* pp.16-25.

19. Wilkinson and Frost, *Thinking Clearly about God and Science,* p.412.

20. John Polkinghorne, *Quarks, Chaos and Christianity,* Triangle, pp.82-3 (emphasis added).

21. *The Times,* 13 July 1984 (emphasis added).

22. Philip Schaff, *History of the Christian Church,* vol. 1, Charles Scribner's Sons, p.175.

23. Cited by Edgar Powell, *On Giant's Shoulders,* Day One Publications, p.168.

24. Romans 1:4.

25. Romans 1:4 — The Amplified Bible, Zondervan Publishing House.

26. Paul Althaus, *Die Wahrheit des kirchlichen Osterglaubens.*

27. The soldiers were under the governor's orders to break the victims' legs (the usual *coup de grâce*) and would not have dared to disobey, but in the case of Jesus the text clearly tells us that there was no need to do this because they 'found that he was already dead' (John 19:33). However, to make doubly sure (or as a last vicious gesture?) one of the soldiers rammed his spear into Jesus' side, 'bringing a sudden flow of blood and water' (John 19:34).

There are at least two viable explanations of what the text is describing. When a dying person's heart stops bleeding the blood inside the heart chambers clots fairly quickly, then separates into parts, the plasma and the blood cells. A stab in the region of the heart and lungs with a typical Roman spear would produce a mixture of the two, something a layman might well describe as 'blood and water'. The second explanation is based on the fact that the terrible trauma Jesus suffered before and during crucifixion would almost certainly have caused a build-up of fluid in the pericardial sac surrounding the heart, as well as enlarging the heart chambers with blood. If the spear had pierced these two organs within ten minutes of Jesus' death, while the blood was still very fluid, the result would have been the 'sudden flow of blood and water' described by John. Whatever the exact pathological explanation, the Bible's words have an impressive ring of truth about them, and help to confirm the fact that Jesus was dead.

28. See John 19:39.

29. D. F. Strauss, *The Life of Jesus for the People,* vol. 1, Williams & Norgate, p.412.

30. Luke 23:55.

31. J. N. D. Anderson, *Jesus Christ: The Witness of History,* InterVarsity Press, p.129.

32. Andrew Fairbairn, *Studies in the Life of Christ.*

33. Charles A. Colson, *Kingdoms in Conflict,* Zondervan, p.70.

34. Anderson, *Jesus Christ: The Witness of History,* p.146.

35. See Mark 16:9; Matthew 28:9; Luke 24:15-32,34,36; John 20:26; John 21:1-23; 1 Corinthians 15:6,7; Matthew 28:18; Luke 24:50-51.

36. 1 Corinthians 15:6.

37. Mark 16:11.

38. Mark 16:5.

39. Arthur Rendle Short, *Why Believe?*, InterVarsity Press, p.51.
40. D. James Kennedy, *The Gates of Hell Shall Not Prevail*, Thomas Nelson Publishers, p.21.
41. Cited by Wilbur M. Smith, *Therefore Stand: Christian Apologetics*, Baker Book House, p.425.
42. See John Warwick Montgomery, *The Law Above the Law*, Bethany, p.132.
43. Simon Greenleaf, *Testimony of the Evangelists, Examined by the Rules of Evidence Administered in Courts of Justice*, Baker Book House, p.46.
44. Cited by Erwin H. Linton, *A Lawyer Examines the Bible: A Defence of the Christian Faith*, Creation Life Publishers, p.xxiv.
45. Cited by Michael Green, *Man Alive!*, Inter-Varsity Fellowship, p.54.
46. See Mark 13:19.
47. See Mark 12:28-30.
48. See John 10:35.
49. See Matthew 12:39-41; 24:37-39.
50. See Matthew 15:4; Mark 12:36.
51. John 5:39.
52. See, e.g., Matthew 25:31-46.
53. 1 Peter 1:23.
54. Albert Einstein, 'Science and Religion', *Out of my Later Years,* cited by Rhoda Thomas Tripp, *The International Thesaurus of Quotations,* George Allan & Unwin, p.564.

Chapter 6 — Lazy fatheads?

1. See www.rationalist.org.uk.
2. Peter Atkins, *Free Inquiry Magazine,* vol. 18, no.2.
3. See *Daily Telegraph,* 6 April 1998.
4. See www.infidels.org.library/modern/peteratkins.html.
5. See J. H. Leuba, *The Belief in God and Immortality: A Psychological, Anthropological and Statistical Survey,* Sherman, French & Co.
6. *Nature,* vol. 386, pp.435-6.
7. See *Nature,* vol. 394, No. 6691, p.313.
8. Psalm 102:25-27.
9. R. Hookyaas, *Religion and the Rise of Modern Science,* Scottish Academic Press, p.9.
10. *US News & World Report,* 16 June 1997.
11. See www.rae.org/believe.html.
12. Henry M. Morris, *Men of Science — Men of God,* Master Books, p.2.
13. *Ibid.,* p.11.
14. Cited by Morris, *Men of Science — Men of God,* p.15.
15. F. Bacon, *The Advancement of Learning,* cited by A. R. Peacocke, *Creation and the World of Science,* Oxford University Press, p.3.
16. Cited by Morris, *Men of Science — Men of God,* p.13.

17. See Dan Graves, *Scientists of Faith,* Kregel Publications, p.57.

18. Cited *ibid.,* p.57.

19. Cited *ibid.,* p.58.

20. www.zapatoni.net.

21. Robert Boyle, *Some Physico-Theological Considerations about the Possibility of the Resurrection,* 1675, University Microfilms International, 15:15, 1981, 36.

22. Cited by Graves, *Scientists of Faith,* p.63.

23. Cited *ibid.,* p.66.

24. Cited by Morris, *Men of Science — Men of God,* p.26.

25. Isaac Newton, *Philosophiae Principia Mathematica,* cited by Holder, *Nothing but Atoms and Molecules,* pp.60-61.

26. Cited by Graves, *Scientists of Faith,* p.82.

27. Cited by Morris, *Men of Science — Men of Faith,* p.37.

28. Cited by I. Asimov, *Biographical Encyclopaedia of Science and Technology: The Lives and Achievements of More than 1000 Great Scientists from Ancient Greece to the Space Age,* Doubleday & Co., p.399.

29. Cited by J. G. Crowther, *British Scientists of the Nineteenth Century,* Routledge & Kegan Paul, p.139.

30. J. P. Joule in a brief autobiography written in January 1863. Published in *Memoirs and Proceedings of the Manchester Literary and Philosophical Society,* vol. LXXV (1930-1931), No. 8, p.110.

31. Cited by Graves, *Scientists of Faith,* p.146.

32. Cited by Colin A. Russell, 'The Conflict Metaphor and its Social Origin', *Science and Christian Belief,* vol. 1, April 1989, p.26.

33. Lord Kelvin, *Victorian Institutes,* No. 124, p.267.

34. Cited by Morris, *Men of Science — Men of Faith,* p.67.

35. Cited by Wilkinson and Frost, *Thinking Clearly about God and Science,* p.203.

36. Cited by Graves, *Scientists of Faith,* p.153.

37. Richard Dawkins, televised debate, reported in *Journal of Alternative Realities,* vol. 7, No. 1, 1999.

38. Michael J. Williams and J. P. Moreland, *Jesus Under Fire,* Paternoster Press, p.10.

39. See www.answersingenesis.org

40. *Ibid.* (I have taken the liberty of formalizing the wording of the interview, without at any point altering the sense of what was said.)

41. Private letter to the author, 3 November 1998.

42. Abridged from Russell, *Science and Christian Belief,* pp.3-26.

Chapter 7 — Beyond science

1. See David Horrobin, *The Journal of the American Botanical Council,* Issue 58, p.72.

2. David Horrobin, *Science is God,* Medical and Technical Publishing Co. Ltd, p.163.

3. *Ibid.,* p.83.

4. Roy Peacock, 'Credibility and Credo', in *Real Science, Real Faith,* ed. Berry, p.33.

5. Johnson, *Testing Darwinism,* p.25.

6. *Ibid.,* p.33.

7. *Daily Telegraph,* 12 April 1996.

8. Cited by Wright, *Designer Universe,* p.61.

9. www.rae.org

10. Lee Spetner, *Not by Chance,* The Judaica Press Inc., p.160.

11. *Independent,* 27 December 1995.

12. Russell, *Why I am not a Christian,* pp.115-16.

13. *Observer,* 19 February 1995.

14. Richard Dawkins, *The Selfish Gene,* Oxford University Press, p.21.

15. Steve Pinker, *How the Mind Works,* Norton, p.52.

16. Richard Dawkins, *Unweaving the Rainbow,* Allen Lane / The Penguin Press, p.ix.

17. Peter Lewis, *The Message of the Living God*, InterVarsity Press, p.99.

18. Woody Allen, *Love and Death'*, cited by Lewis, *The Message of the Living God,* p.15.

19. Woody Allen, 'Death' (a play), in *Without Feathers.*

20. Psalm 19:1.

21. Birkett, *Unnatural Enemies,* pp.60-61.

22. Romans 1:20.

23. Cited by White and Comnellis, *Darwin's Demise,* p.182.

24. See Blanchard, *Does God Believe in Atheists?,* pp.389-412, 447-69.

25. 1 Peter 1:23.

26. Deuteronomy 33:27.

27. Psalm 90:2.

28. James 1:17.

29. Ephesians 1:11.

30. Job 37:16.

31. Habakkuk 1:13.

32. 1 John 1:5.

33. James P. Boyce, *Abstract of Systematic Theology,* reprinted by Christian Gospel Foundation, p.93.

34. 1 John 4:8 (emphasis added).

35. Psalm 18:50.

36. Psalm 31:21.

37. *Playboy,* October 1965.

38. Cited in *Leadership* magazine, Spring 1999, p.75.

39. Ephesians 3:18,19.

40. John 1:18.

41. *Ibid.*
42. Colossians 2:9.
43. Cited by Wilkinson and Frost, *Thinking Clearly about God & Science,* p.190.
44. *Daily Telegraph,* 10 February 2004.
45. Quoted with the author's permission.
46. John 1:14.
47. John 3:16.
48. 1 Timothy 1:15.
49. Romans 3:23.
50. Romans 6:23.
51. Revelation 21:27.
52. Romans 5:8.
53. Matthew 27:46.
54. R. A. Cole, *The Gospel According to Mark, Tyndale New Testament Commentaries,* Tyndale Press, p.243.
55. Galatians 2:20.
56. 1 Peter 3:18.
57. 1 John 3:16.
58. Acts 1:3.
59. 1 Corinthians 8:6.
60. Hebrews 11:6.
61. James 2:19.
62. Matthew 8:29.
63. Mark 1:24.
64. Romans 5:1 (emphasis added).
65. C. S. Lewis, *The World's Last Night,* Harcourt, Brace, p.26.
66. Colin Humphreys, 'Can Science and Christianity Both be True?', in *Real Science, Real Faith,* ed. Berry, p.113.
67. Birkett, *Unnatural Enemies,* p.135.
68. Ephesians 2:12.
69. Romans 1:20.
70. Cited by John Blanchard, *Sifted Silver,* Evangelical Press, p.110.
71. Cited by Charles T. Glicksberg, *Literature and Religion,* Southern Methodist University Press, pp.221-2.
72. Douglas Coupland, *Life After God,* Pocket Star.
73. Acts 17:30.
74. Hebrews 7:25.
75. Werner Heisenberger, *JASA* 37 (December 1985), pp.231-2.
76. Proverbs 2:3-4.

Appendix — The strange story of Christian Science
1. *The New International Dictionary of the Christian Church,* ed. J. D. Douglas, p.328.

2. Ruth Tucker, *Another Gospel*, p.152.
3. Matthew 9:2-8.
4. See Anthony Hoekema, *Christian Science*, Eerdmans, pp.12-23.
5. Mary Baker Eddy, *Science and Health*, p.1 (emphasis added).
6. Cited at http://automatic writing.com/Chapter 4.
7. Paris Flammonde, *The Mystic Healers*.
8. 1 Peter 1:23.
9. Eddy, *Science and Health*, p.99.
10. Psalm 103:19.
11. Mary Baker Eddy, *Miscellaneous Writings*, p.16.
12. Eddy, *Science and Health*, p.113.
13. Eddy, *Miscellaneous Writings*, p.13.
14. See, e.g., Isaiah 64:8.
15. See e.g., Colossians 2:9.
16. See e.g., Genesis 1:2.
17. Eddy, *Science and Health*, p.256.
18. 1 John 5:20.
19. *Science and Health*, p.473.
20. See 2 Corinthians 3:17.
21. Cited by J. Oswald Sanders, *Heresies Ancient and Modern*, p.47.
22. John 4:24.
23. Genesis 1:1.
24. Eddy, *Science and Health*, p.468.
25. e.g., Romans 3:23; Matthew 8:16.
26. Hebrews 9:27.
27. Cited by Sanders, *Heresies Ancient and Modern*, p.48.
28. Eddy, *Science and Health*, p.283.
29. *Ibid.*, p.377.
30. See 1 Peter 3:18.
31. Cited by Sanders, *Heresies Ancient and Modern*, p.48.
32. See Acts 1:11.
33. See Matthew 5:22.
34. Cited by Sanders, *Heresies Ancient and Modern*, p.49.
35. *Ibid.*

Index

A wide range of excellent books on spiritual subjects is available from Evangelical Press. Please write to us for your free catalogue or contact us by e-mail.

Evangelical Press
Faverdale North Industrial Estate, Darlington, Co. Durham, DL3 0PH, England

Evangelical Press USA
P. O. Box 825, Webster, New York 14580, USA

e-mail: sales@evangelicalpress.org

web: http://www.evangelicalpress.org